PREHISPANIC AMERICA

ST. MARTIN'S SERIES IN PREHISTORY

*Shirley Gorenstein and Robert Stigler,
General Editors*

PREHISPANIC AMERICA
THE OLD WORLD: EARLY MAN TO THE DEVELOPMENT
OF AGRICULTURE

Forthcoming:

NORTH AMERICA
VARIETIES OF CULTURE IN THE OLD WORLD
A HISTORY OF AMERICAN ARCHAEOLOGY:
METHOD AND THEORY

PREHISPANIC AMERICA

Shirley Gorenstein
Richard G. Forbis
Paul Tolstoy
Edward P. Lanning

under the editorial supervision of
Shirley Gorenstein

St. Martin's Press   New York

Library of Congress Catalog Card Number: 74-77529
Copyright © 1974 by St. Martin's Press, Inc.
All Rights Reserved.
Manufactured in the United States of America.
For information, write: St. Martin's Press, Inc.,
175 Fifth Avenue, New York, N.Y. 10010

AFFILIATED PUBLISHERS: Macmillan Limited, London—
also at Bombay, Calcutta, Madras, and Melbourne

The editors dedicate this series to
William Duncan Strong
who provided a standard of excellence
toward which his students continue to strive

PREFACE

This volume is one of a series whose aims are to give a succinct introduction to the study of prehistory and to sum up the present state of knowledge concerning prehistoric cultural developments in the significant archaeological areas of the Old and New Worlds.

The study of prehistory has been going on in an organized way for more than one hundred years. The results have been presented in thousands of papers, monographs, and books. Indeed, by the beginning of this century the amount of published information had become so vast that archaeologists found it hard to be prehistorians of the world. Space and time were divided up, and researchers became specialists in certain geographical areas and sometimes in certain periods. In recent years it has become even more difficult for one archaeologist to write a global prehistory. The would-be generalist today is hard-put to keep abreast of a whole field which is subject to radical technical and theoretical advances as well as a continuing explosion of information. Furthermore, the archaeologist always has a tendency to favor the area or areas where he has worked and to slight others of which he has no first-hand knowledge.

To overcome these problems, we have arranged for each of the first four books in this series to be written by a team of several authors, all of them specialists in one or more regions or time periods. The author of each chapter had a free hand, subject to limitations of space, in presenting his view of the present state of archaeological knowledge in his area. In none of the volumes or chapters has there been any effort to impose a Procrustean uniformity, other than in the general length and depth of treatment given to coordinate subjects. The authors have subscribed, however, to an overall organizational plan which is meant to give the series coherence as well as balance. This plan is primarily geographical, though some volumes and chapters also have temporal and topical aspects. The final book of the series, written by one of the editors with an introduction by the other, will be a history of archaeological method and theory in America.

We are indebted to Barry Rossinoff, who conceived the format of the series and saw the books' preparation through tumultuous times. We are also grateful to Judy Hammond, who worked with intelligence as well as artistry in preparing the drawings, and to Brian Hesse, who was an innovative and indefatigable research assistant on the project.

SHIRLEY GORENSTEIN
ROBERT STIGLER

CONTENTS

INTRODUCTION
SHIRLEY GORENSTEIN

Archaeologists studying prehistoric times have set themselves the task of finding out what man's life was like before writing enabled him to be his own witness. Instead of writing, archaeologists use other kinds of evidence—namely, material things that have lasted until the present. They are artifactual, physical, anthropological, geological, botanical, zoological. Woven together they give the shape and content of past culture, and they also lead to interpretations about how cultures have changed, why they take one direction rather than another, and why some are alike and others different.

But a straightforward plan of investigation has always been easier to design than to execute. The data are not always sufficient, they sometimes do not fit together, they require a number of kinds of analysis before they are intelligible, and often they may serve equally well for different or even opposing conclusions. An archaeologist's interpretation depends upon what he was after in the first place. Did he want to explain how culture changes, or was he more interested in showing the historical relationships between particular cultures?

This book is concerned with the prehistory of the southern part of the New World, from "nuclear" America (roughly comprising Mexico, Central America, and parts of northern and western South America) to the tip of the Southern Hemisphere. These are areas where what is called "civilization" evolved and where simple cultures thrived as well. The authors of the following chapters give

1

an account of what happened in the past as well as why it happened. As scholars always must, they take into account the fragility of the data; and they are aware of the philosophical assumptions and interests shaping their interpretations.

Richard Forbis begins his chapter, "The Paleoamericans," by turning to the physical anthropological evidence concerning the origin of man in the New World. He makes two important points initially. The first is that man was an *immigrant* to the New World. Since, aside from man, the New World contains no living or fossil primate more highly evolved than the monkey, there is no reason to think that man evolved independently here. The second point relates to the physical anthropological evidence on *when* man came to the New World. Since all fossil relics of man found in the New World have been of the species *Homo sapiens,* it seems that man must have arrived here after *Homo sapiens* evolved in the Old World about 40,000 years ago.

Homo sapiens has itself evolved, however (though not to the extent of forming a new species), and Forbis goes on to offer the evidence on the earlier and later forms of men in the New World. This evidence has forced archaeologists to lay aside at least one simplistic notion: the idea that, since native Americans at the time of the European conquest were Mongoloid in appearance, the original migrants must have been Mongoloid. The Mongoloid characteristics, the evidence now indicates, are probably a late development and do not tell us anything about the initial migration.

Archaeologists concerned with *how* man migrated from the Old to the New World and through the New World from Alaska to the tip of South America have turned to the geological evidence. Much controversy has centered, for instance, on the dating of glacial advances and retreats, which supposedly determined when man was able to enter the new continent. Forbis cuts through these arguments by pointing out that neither the glaciers nor Bering Strait set up such formidable barriers as archaeologists once thought. Migrations could have taken place under many kinds of environmental circumstances.

As Forbis shows, the best evidence we have about early culture in Mexico, Central America, and South America comes from a time in the Pleistocene when men were engaged in hunting big game.

Most of the tools found are related to this activity. They are projectile points used in killing animals and knives, scrapers, and awls used in butchering and preparing the skins. But the dates that are associated with these tools are late Pleistocene, and most archaeologists agree that man came to the New World several thousand years earlier.

The evidence from the earlier time periods is sketchy or unsubstantiated. There is not enough information to describe a standard tool kit that may have been used. It may be, of course, that there was at this time no hemisphere-wide standardization in the manufacture of stone tools. As Forbis remarks in his summary, more sites and a greater precision of dating are needed before definite conclusions can be drawn about the "pre-projectile point stage."

Archaeologists are on considerably firmer ground for the period following the Pleistocene projectile point horizon. Forbis introduces the reader to the substantial body of information gathered from Mexico and South America. Here the beginning of diversification in culture can be seen—the adaptation of man to changed environmental niches. In the chapters following Forbis', the account of adaptation and cultural development is continued.

The level of culture that archaeologists call "civilization" developed in two places in the New World: Mesoamerica and western South America. "Civilization," as Lanning describes it in "The Transformation to Civilization," refers to a complex society which has a well-developed agricultural base and large, densely settled populations that are economically and socially stratified. There is also a political authority which controls aspects of intracommunity life as well as intercommunity relations. This definition applies both to Mesoamerica and to western South America and indeed to other early civilizations such as those found in Mesopotamia, Egypt, and China. In other words, these societies were all organized in much the same way, though they varied in such matters as the type of crop cultivated.

Paul Tolstoy begins his chapter "Mesoamerica" by referring to Kirchhoff's classic article enumerating that civilization's distinctive traits. The study of the distribution of these traits in space and time established the boundaries of Mesoamerica—extending from central Mexico to Costa Rica and from the period of 1200 B.C. to the Spanish Conquest.

But Tolstoy also takes note of the time before 1200 B.C., partly for historical reasons, but more importantly for anthropological reasons. While he is interested in the particular antecedents of the Mesoamerican economy, he is more concerned with its shifting character, with the process of change from a hunting and gathering economy, which cannot support the complexities of civilization, to an agricultural economy, which is a necessary condition for civilization. Study of the process can reveal why some societies undergo the transformation to civilization while others do not.

Yet the development of civilization can hardly be described as a single line—one community walking unerringly down a lonely path. Implicit in Tolstoy's discussion is the notion that civilization is the product of the interaction of many communities. The distribution of Olmec traits or of Olmec influence in other parts of Mexico is important in this context. Studying the distribution, we can see that various microenvironmental zones were being tapped; we can then begin to understand how certain mechanisms brought the communities in those zones into an economic network of mutual dependency.

Tolstoy touches on the argument about whether Olmec can be called a "civilization." Because it appeared earlier than complex societies of the Classic and Postclassic, some archaeologists have insisted it must have had a simpler form. But that is confusing chronology with evolution. Olmec appears earlier on a chronological chart, but it can be put in the same stage as later cultures on an evolutionary scale. Perhaps it would be best not to use stages at all, but to give traits of societies different values and range them on a continuum. If that were done, Olmec would surely fall closer to the complex than to the simple end of the continuum. Therefore, without quarreling over the use of the particular term "civilization," we can recognize, as Tolstoy does, that Olmec society was a spectacular innovation. It launched not only the Mesoamerican tradition but also the new and more complex organization of society that lasted until the Spanish Conquest.

Most of the rest of Mesoamerica at the time of Olmec consisted of simpler communities. They were not, however, without a rich cultural content and great economic potential. The work on Tla-tilco done by Tolstoy and a number of other archaeologists has revealed the chronological, stylistic, and ritual dimensions of this Valley of Mexico culture. Archaeological investigations in other parts of Mesoamerica have uncovered what might be called the base culture on which Olmec influence acted to form particular regional expressions.

In the Classic period, which began about A.D. 250, there was a florescence of cultural complexity throughout Mesoamerica. The variability that Tolstoy demonstrates in the forms of the Classic societies—all clearly civilizations—has been a major theoretical concern of Mesoamerican archaeologists. The two areas that show the greatest contrast are the central highlands and the southern low-lands. The highland society of Teotihuacán differs from the Low-land Maya societies such as Tikal in certain critical characteristics, particularly population size and density. Teotihuacán, which Tol-stoy discusses at length, covered in its heyday an area of 20 square kilometers and had a population of 85,000 or perhaps as many as 125,000. Tikal, on the other hand, covered an area of 64 square kilometers with a population of from 20,000 to 39,000. Moreover, at Teotihuacán there was considerable occupational specialization and a grading in possession of wealth, while at Tikal the popula-tion was more polarized into an elite and a plebeian class. These differences and others like them have been linked by various scholars with the environmental contexts of the societies: in the highlands the interaction of environment and culture produced an economic system that could support a large stable population in a limited area, while in the lowlands a vast amount of land and a mobile population were required.

There was a faltering of Classic communities in the second half of the first millennium A.D. The forms of civilization that had de-veloped apparently were not capable of handling the growth of the communities. By A.D. 900 new, more appropriate forms emerged. Tolstoy shows how they were characterized by a stronger military-political system than had existed in the previous societies. Though the Mixteca-Puebla region was somewhat loosely linked politically and unspecialized militarily, the Toltecs, the Tlaxcalans, the Ta-rascans, and the Aztecs all demonstrated increasing political cen-

tralization and military specialization. And yet, as Tolstoy points
out, there was never any complete, monolithic control over Mesoamerica as there was in western South America.

The chapter "Western South America," by Edward P. Lanning,
provides the reader not only with a culture history of that area but
with an interpretation based on the idea that the adaptation of man
to the particular environmental circumstances of the area limited
and directed his cultural choices.

For the early post-Pleistocene period Lanning describes a pattern of seasonal exploitation of different environmental zones. At
this time the availability of food was in the hands of nature rather
than of man, and the schedule of nature therefore directed man's
schedule. Ultimately, the domestication of plants and animals gave
man a control over his life that could never have been obtained
while he followed the vagaries of nature. Yet, as the culture history
reveals, there is no simple cause-and-effect relationship between
domestication and societal complexity but rather a complicated association among many variables. Adaptation to a beneficent environment could produce sedentary villages; on the other hand,
knowledge of domestication did not always result in the abandonment of hunting and gathering, and societies could cultivate some
plants while remaining essentially nomadic.

Lanning shows that by the second millennium B.C. there was full-
time farming, and large, dense populations lived in settlements that
had public buildings as well as residences. A different kind of community organization was forming, one that Lanning calls the Rural
Nucleated state. There was now specialization in economic, political, and religious life. At the same time certain technological in-
novations were coming into Peru, apparently from northern South
America: pottery-making and weaving. The next millennium saw
the development of this cultural configuration in central and north
central Peru.

It is in the context of the changing organization of society that
Lanning evaluates the Chavín cult and art style, which dominated
the culture history of the first millennium before Christ. The study
of the characteristics of the Chavín art style has enabled archaeologists to plot the spread of Chavín throughout the coast and highlands of northern and central Peru. There is, however, less concern

with why Chavín moved across Peru than with its effect. Whatever the desires of the Chavín priests (if they did exist) and whatever the satisfactions of the converts (if there were any), when Chavín touched new areas it left, in addition to the characteristics of its style and cult, the form of complex society that it represented. This form became fixed in western South America.

After the waning of Chavín, a new development, which Lanning calls the Urban state, appeared in previously quiescent southern Peru. Large, dense populations were living and working in settlements characterized not only by occupational specialization and public as well as residential buildings but also by dependence upon an economic exchange with the hinterland. Lanning sees population growth and the consequent demand for a greater food supply as the key to the opening up of new farmland and the close linkage of the rural population with the city in the Synchoritic Urban form of organization. Irrigation canals, invented earlier, now became a major technological improvement which increased the productivity of the land.

At this time there were different kinds of settlement (city and village), a symbiotic relationship between them, and a concentration in one place of political power that extended over large areas. It was this last characteristic that became most pronounced during the further developments in western South America. In the middle of the first millennium A.D. empire-building began to occur, as Huari, Tiahuanaco, and Pachacamac began to incorporate contiguous territory by increasingly sophisticated political and military means. In a certain sense that was the final organizational change in the culture of the area. From then on the shifts were purely historical; empires fell and new ones replaced them, but few changes were made in the type of political and military system that had launched empire-building. The Incas, however, with whom Lanning ends the chapter on western South America, varied from the earlier empires in their rural form of organization. There was no great Inca capital city, even though there was an Inca capital. The Incas were able to acquire the political and military systems of the Urban states and fix them, perhaps shakily, on a rural base. The Inca empire was like an imperfectly grafted plant and, for this reason, died at just the touch of the Spanish sword.

A question of major concern to archaeologists working in the New World has been why civilization develops in one area and not in another. Certainly the South American continent would seem to be an ideal place to pursue this line of inquiry, for there the Andean mountain range draws a firm line between the west, where civilization developed, and the east, where it did not. Unfortunately, as Lanning notes in the next chapter, "Eastern South America," the prehistory of the eastern area is not well known because climatic and geological processes have destroyed and buried the sites and vegetation now obscures them. Perhaps even more important is the fact that there apparently were no spectacular buildings or earthworks as there were in the west, and smaller sites are always difficult to discover.

Archaeologists working in the area are concerned with establishing very basic culture history. Referring to ceramic and other material evidence, Lanning summarizes what is presently known or inferred about the content of the cultures and the migration of peoples from one area to another. From this summary two basic points emerge. The first is the existence of cultural stability as opposed to the accelerated cultural change seen in the areas where civilization developed. The second, related to the first, is the lack of much response to the stimuli provided by both Mesoamerica and the Andean area. These points should not be surprising: homeostasis is a powerful force and is more characteristic of cultural systems than is disequilibrium. It is not, then, eastern South America that is remarkable but rather Mesoamerica and western South America, where dislocation and change did occur.

In "The Transformation to Civilization" Lanning addresses himself to the processes by which civilization emerged in those areas of the New World where it did come into being. He begins with a definition of "civilization." One difficulty for New World scholars is that most previous definitions of the term have been appropriate only for the Old World, where archaeology got its start as a discipline some hundred years ago. Moreover, definitions have tended to allow too little variety: civilization has been seen as a single "culture type" or a "form of society." Some complex societies have therefore not fit the definitions; they have been lumped with simple cultures with which they do not properly belong, or they have been admitted to the narrow "civilization" category only as awkward exceptions to the general rule. Lanning suggests that civilization is not a single form. Developing the terms he used in "Western South America," he suggests two main varieties: the Synchoritic Urban and the Rural Nucleated. In addition, he points out that the cultures of Colombia and Ecuador, previously thought to be complex but not yet "civilization," may be a third variety—namely, the Achoritic Urban.

Having defined types of civilization, Lanning turns to what is for him the major question: how complex society came into being. He identifies social stratification and central authority as the key traits of emerging civilization, and he then looks for the causes of these critical effects. He finds them in the interaction of two fortuitous circumstances: the pressure of population growth and the scarcity of basic resources. In such circumstances societies had to reorganize in order to survive. The shift to a centrally organized, stratified society may not have been the only possible solution, but it is one that has been invented independently again and again in different parts of the world. The new societies were able to grow in a direction unavailable to the old.

Lanning goes on to discuss briefly the evolution of civilization in various parts of Mesoamerica and Peru. He does not let the abstract concept of evolution become an oversimplification of the complexity of a civilization's actual development; on the contrary, he focuses on variation in particular societies.

In the final chapter of the book, Paul Tolstoy deals with the idea of transoceanic diffusion: the possible spread of cultural traits from the Old World to the New. Since the inception of archaeology as a discipline, diffusion and evolution have usually been treated as mutually exclusive explanations of cultural change: *either* a certain trait evolved within a society, *or* it was borrowed from another society with which the first came in contact. Although evolution and diffusion are presented here in separate chapters, there is no such dichotomy between the two processes. Both evolution and diffusion can play roles in the formation of society.

To establish that diffusion has occurred, an archaeologist must first show that there was contact between two cultures. There must be a similarity between the material remains in the two places, a similarity that cannot be explained by the "psychic unity of man" or by the effects of the same environmental zone. Although the strongest evidence for diffusion is that an item made or produced in one place is found in another, contact can of course occur without objects themselves being carried from one place to another. It is obvious, too, that shared complexes of artifacts or attributes are stronger evidence of connection than a few shared objects or traits. What Tolstoy has done in his article "Transoceanic Diffusion and Nuclear America" is to list the various items, traits, and complexes that show a correspondence between the New World and the Old. At this stage in the development of our knowledge, the evidence for diffusion is not definitive, but it is solid enough that it cannot be ignored or entirely explained away. Tolstoy has taken on the responsibility of presenting this evidence and of pointing out that tests should be applied to discover whether the cultural similarities are indeed the result of diffusion.

If diffusion did occur, what was its role in the development of the early civilizations of the New World? Certainly, it would have played *some* part, Tolstoy answers. While it may be true that New World civilizations were the result of adaptation to natural and cultural environment, it is also true that some elements in that environment may well have come from outside.

The phenomenon of cultural change is the focus of this book's attention. No aspect of this change is more troublesome and more fascinating than the development of civilization. The articles in this book are intended to give readers the substantive data on the long culture history of part of the New World and also to suggest explanations of why cultural transformations came about. Of course, no book can include all the interpretations that have been promulgated within the discipline. There is no consensus among prehistorians working in this field or, indeed, in any other. But the authors of this book think of the many controversies as a sign of strength rather than weakness. Debate is often the mark of a vital and growing branch of knowledge.

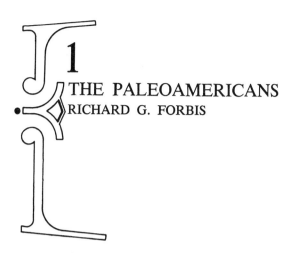

1
THE PALEOAMERICANS
RICHARD G. FORBIS

Archaeologists generally agree that the earliest Americans crossed over Bering Strait from Asia. This agreement is virtually unique because stimulating debates rage over most other questions concerning the first settlers of the New World.

On a physical level, attempts to show that man evolved from prosimian ancestors in the New World have proved fruitless. While prosimians did indeed live in the New World at the beginning of the Tertiary (some 80 million years ago or more), they soon disappeared from all but South and Middle America, where they gave rise only to the New World monkeys. There was no further evolution toward man. Early hominids that may be transitional to modern man, such as *Australopithecus* and *Homo erectus,* remained restricted to the Old World. All fossil men so far recovered in the Americas are of the modern immigrant species, *Homo sapiens.*

Attempts to define the race of *Homo sapiens* to which the Paleoamericans belonged have proved inconclusive. While the Indians at the time of the first European contact possessed strong Mongoloid features, the earliest occupants of South America appear to have been physically distinctive. Widely distributed in early contexts is the "Lagoa Santa type" of skull, which is characterized by a long head, a slightly projecting face, a low forehead, and prominent cheekbones. Though most common in Brazil, similar skulls have been identified from Ecuador and Patagonia. Later finds show increasing traces of Mongoloid characteristics, perhaps as a result of

11

subsequent migrations from Asia or perhaps as a result of evolution, parallel to that in eastern Asia but slower.

Inasmuch as *Homo sapiens* could conceivably extend back hundreds of thousands of years in the Old World, physical anthropology is not particularly helpful in pinpointing the time of man's arrival in the New. This question is more likely to be answered by prehistory archaeologists. Even here, no ultimate solution will ever be found. The maximum age demonstrated by incontrovertible proof must never be regarded as anything more than the minimum age of man's first conquest of the New World.

In reconstructing early prehistory, archaeologists lean heavily upon other sciences for evidence, not only of age, but of past environments. Geologically, the Pleistocene (or Glacial) epoch can be defined as the Age of Man, and it apparently began about 3 million years ago. But this definition applies only to the Old World. Man arrived late in North America, perhaps during the Wisconsin (or final) glaciation, which began a mere 70,000 years ago. The glacial masses were highly unstable, and Wisconsin ice fluctuated many times, flowing out during stades and retreating during interstades. Early fluctuations are poorly defined, but the "Classical" Wisconsin reached its maximum about 20,000 years ago and then tapered off. Apparently the glaciers in the Andes of South America followed much the same pattern. Pluvials—periods of heavy rainfall—are often thought to have been synchronous with glaciations, and pluvial deposits at lower elevations in South America have sometimes offered the key to dating archaeological sites.

Speculations that the North American glaciers fused to form an ice barrier that existed for thousands of years and sealed off the passage south from Alaska have little or no basis in fact. Nor was it necessary for early migrants to wait for the Bering land bridge to appear and link the Old World to the New. This bridge was in part contemporaneous with glacial maxima, when water locked up on land in the form of ice resulted in lowered sea-levels, exposing the relatively shallow shelf now under Bering Strait. While there are different opinions, it does not seem likely that man had to depend on the emergence of Beringia before entering the New World. Bering Strait is not a formidable obstacle. Quite the opposite, it is a hunter's paradise, abounding in fish, sea mammals, and land mammals grazing on the bordering coastal tundras and grasslands. Even now, the narrow strait occasionally freezes over and is passable on foot. Once established in Alaska, man found no insuperable obstacles to his movement to the southern tip of South America.

In conjunction with the following sections, the reader should refer to Maps 1.1 and 1.2 and Chart 1.1.

· SOUTH AMERICA

The Pleistocene Projectile Point Horizon
In South America there is clear evidence of early hunters of now extinct animals—native horse and ground sloth—as well as guanaco. A number of sites have yielded artifacts which were used by these hunters. In the earliest assemblage, from Fell's Cave in southern Patagonia, projectile points are generally stemmed ("fish tail") rather than lanceolate like early point types in North America (Figure 1.1). In addition Fell's Cave yielded unique discoidal stones, big side scrapers, and bone tools useful in processing animal bones, hides, and flesh. The lowest occupation level with human cremations has been dated 8770 B.C. ± 300 and 9050 B.C. ± 170.

Elsewhere in South America, Fell's Cave points have been reported from Argentina, where they occur in the Toldense complex, which also includes bola stones and discoidal stones as well as human remains and the bone of a native horse. There are stray finds of Fell's Cave points from Brazil and Uruguay, but the largest group of artifacts comes from El Inga, near Quito, Ecuador, some 4,300 miles from Fell's Cave (Figure 1.1). There, artifacts of different ages and affiliations were mixed, and the earliest radiocarbon date of 7080 B.C. ± 144 is not necessarily the age of the initial occupation. In the Huanta complex of highland Peru, which contains extinct deer and possibly horse bones, Fell's Cave points are dated some one to two thousand years earlier.

Other evidence for early man in South America on about the same time level as Fell's Cave comes from Tagua Tagua, Chile, where flakes, knives, and bone implements date to 9430 B.C. ± 320. The site has yielded no projectile points as yet, but it shares scraper types with Fell's Cave. It is thought to be the site of a horse and

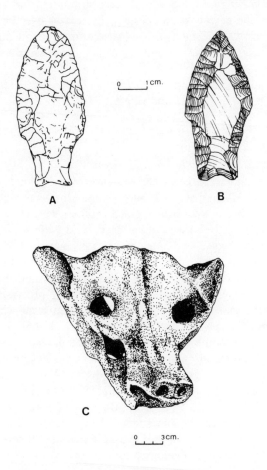

A   B

C

0 ___ 3cm.

Based in part on an illustration in Junius Bird, *A Comparison of South Chilean and Ecuadorian "Fishtail" Projectile Points* (Berkeley: Kroeber Anthropological Society, University of California, 1969), Paper 40.

FIGURE 1.1   *(A)* Fell's Cave projectile point.   *(B)* Fell's Cave projectile point from El Inga.   *(C)* Fossil camelid sacrum from Tequixquiac, carved to represent an animal head.

mastodon kill, but bones of deer, birds, frogs, and fish were also recovered.

Before the Pleistocene Projectile Point Horizon

A "pre-projectile point stage" has been posited by A. D. Krieger and accepted by many Americanists. During this stage, man is thought to have been technologically incapable of producing points or knives of thin, biface form. Stone tools were made by percussion only and were usually large and heavy. Cut, beveled, and worn splinters of bone are said to have served as tools.

Sites revealing such simple assemblages need not necessarily be ancient, since they may represent survivals late in the stage. Stage and age are separate considerations. But some sites, Krieger maintains, "should be considerably earlier than the first projectile points." While a number of sites have been attributed great age on various grounds, most of the attributions are questionable, for these reasons:

1. Frequently the sites are in surface locations, where reliable dating is impossible.
2. Some sites are dated, but the putative artifacts may not be man-made.
3. Some sites are firmly dated to an early period but have yielded such a small sample of artifacts that they cannot convincingly be demonstrated to lack projectile points.
4. Some sites are workshops or quarries. Crudeness of the waste debris left at these stations cannot be accepted as proof of antiquity.
5. Some sites lie in situations suggesting antiquity but have not as yet been dated precisely.

One site assigned to the pre-projectile point horizon escapes these difficulties—the Ayacucho complex from low levels of Piki-machay Cave, Peru, where cultural remains including side scrapers, spokeshaves, and choppers were found buried in association with an extinct giant sloth, *Megatherium,* and a camelid. This site's radiocarbon age, 12200 B.C. ± 180, is about 3,000 years earlier than Fell's Cave. To date, only a small part of the site has been excavated, however, and further digging is needed to permit de-

FIGURE 1.2 Now-extinct mammals of the Pleistocene. *(A)* Camelid or wild llama. *(B)* Columbian elephant. *(C)* Ground sloth *(Megatherium)*. *(D)* Native horse. *(E)* Mastodon.

termination of the place of this early and distinctive complex in South American contexts. At present it remains an archaeological anomaly.

Bones of *Megatherium,* as well as mastodon and extinct horse (Figure 1.2), have come from a bog at Muaco, Venezuela, where dates on burned bones range from 12350 B.C. ± 500 to as late as 7080 B.C. ± 240. The bones are broken and cut, as if by man, but whether they are the same age as some stone artifacts in the bog is unresolved, since even modern glass has slipped in among the bones. A similar fauna, said to be associated with unchipped cobble hammerstones, is dated at nearby Taima Taima to 11060 B.C. ± 280 and 12490 B.C. ± 435. These sites may possibly belong to the pre-projectile point stage since they contain extinct fauna similar to that from Ayacucho.

Near El Jobo, also in Venezuela, some 45 sites have been ordered into sequent phases on the basis of correlations with terraces of the Río Pedregal. The earliest phase, Camare, consists of large bifaces, scrapers, and utilized flakes of quartzite. Camare is followed by Las Lagunas, which, in addition, contains pointed bifaces and side scrapers. On the third lowest terrace, the El Jobo complex, which includes projectile points, is comparatively young. The large proportion of chipping debris from many of these stations suggests that they were essentially workshops or quarry sites.

Chivateros, a quarry in Peru, contains stratified materials considered equivalent to Lagunas. A radiocarbon determination from the top of Chivateros I (under Chivateros II) came to 8480 B.C. ± 160. A still lower formation at the same site, the "Red Zone," yielded thin tabular pieces of rock with steep unifacial flaking on the edges and some flakes and cores. Age estimates place it as far back as 15000 B.C. Oquendo, a nearby site specializing in burins, has been placed on typological grounds between the Red Zone and Chivateros I because it shares artifact types with both. Pertinent radiocarbon dates are few, and it remains to be seen whether these quarries are actually of appreciable antiquity.

After the Pleistocene Projectile Point Horizon
After Fell's Cave points went out of style, there is some evidence that man continued to hunt now extinct animals in South America

MAP 1.1   Early man sites in South America.

with new kinds of tools. Several caves near Lagoa Santa, Brazil, suggest that he probably did, but indisputable proof is lacking. Cerca Grande, dated to 7770 B.C. ± 128, has yielded human remains and crude quartz artifacts, including projectile points. At Confins Cave, human remains may possibly have been associated with extinct horse, mastodon, and wild llama (Figure 1.2), among other animals. Human remains have been reported also from Punin, Ecuador, in an undated fossil-bearing stratum that also contained bones of horse, mastodon, and other Pleistocene animals. At Palli Aike Cave near the Straits of Magellan, stemmed projectile points in association with horse and ground sloth have been dated at 6466 B.C. ± 410 and 6689 B.C. ± 450.

The El Jobo complex proper, mentioned above, is probably also of later age than the Pleistocene projectile point horizon. No animal remains have been preserved, but the projectile points resemble some North American types of post-glacial age. It is tempting to believe that hunters seeking modern species of game animals (deer and camelids) ranged through much of South America, as they did in North America immediately after the Pleistocene extinctions.

The Puente complex of south highland Peru is indicative of hunters of deer and wild llama and may date back almost to 8000 B.C. Puente contains a variety of projectile point types and stone implements that are also found on the west coast in the lower Tres Ventanas Cave and in the northern highlands at Guitarrero Cave, where some radiocarbon dates run back beyond 8000 B.C.

In northwest Argentina willow leaf points, resembling some from Puente, and grinding stones have been found. Here man was not only a hunter of guanaco but also a processor of vegetal foods by about 6000 B.C. He had departed from primary reliance on hunting, and discrete groups were settling into local districts. So, between 8000 B.C. and 6000 B.C., highland hunters seem to have come down from the Andean spine and accommodated themselves, east and west, to other resources in varied settings.

About the same time sea-mammal hunters occupied Englefield Island in the southern extremes of Chile, manifesting still further cultural diversity. They used harpoons as well as projectile points. Except for some traces at Anangula in the Aleutians and Five Mile

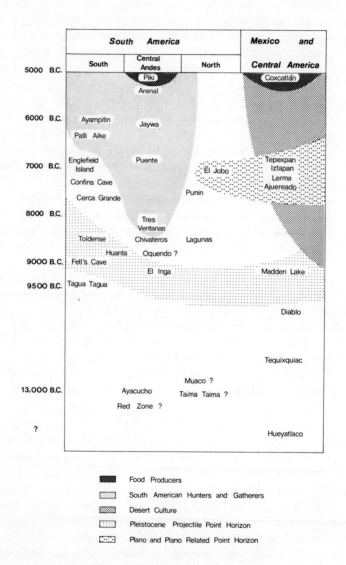

	South America			Mexico and
	South	Central Andes	North	Central America
5000 B.C.		Piki		Coxcatlán
		Arenal		
6000 B.C.	Ayampitin	Jaywa		
	Palli Aike			
7000 B.C.	Englefield Island	Puente	El Jobo	Tepexpan Iztapan Lerma Ajuereado
	Confins Cave			
	Cerca Grande		Punin	
8000 B.C.		Tres Ventanas		
	Toldense	Chivateros	Lagunas	
	Huanta	Oquendo ?		
9000 B.C.	Fell's Cave	El Inga		Madden Lake
9500 B.C.	Tagua Tagua			
				Diablo
				Tequixquiac
13,000 B.C.	Ayacucho	Muaco ? Taima Taima ?		
	Red Zone ?			
?				Hueyatlaco

▓▓▓ Food Producers

░░░ South American Hunters and Gatherers

▒▒▒ Desert Culture

⋯⋯ Pleistocene Projectile Point Horizon

⋯⋯ Plano and Plano Related Point Horizon

CHART 1.1   Paleoamerican culture.

Rapids, Oregon, which may be slightly earlier, evidence of fishing and sea-mammal hunting appears to be absent elsewhere in the seacoasts of the Americas at this time level. Sites may have been drowned or uplifted by coastal warping to positions that have been eroded away.

The Arenal complex of the central coast of Peru is dated at 5330 B.C. ± 120 and 5290 B.C. ± 120. Arenal sites seem to be the camps of transhumant hunters who followed deer and guanaco from the highlands to the *lomas* meadows, which bloomed in winter and provided sustenance to man and animal in the form of seeds and roots. This pattern of seasonal movement was to continue for thousands of years, until climatic changes resulted in the progressive diminution of the *lomas* and the resources of the sea became correspondingly important.

Domestication of plants and animals signals the end of the Paleoamerican period. Incipient agriculture is present possibly before 5500 B.C. in the Jaywa complex of Ayacucho, in highland Peru. Tropical seed plants may have been cultivated and the llama domesticated. In the following Piki complex (5500 B.C.–4300 B.C.) evidence for domestication of plants, such as gourds and quinoa, and of animals, such as the llama and guinea pig, is more positive.

· MEXICO AND CENTRAL AMERICA

The Pleistocene Projectile Point Horizon

A Fell's Cave point has been identified from Madden Lake, Panama. From here it is but a short distance to Guatemala, where a "waisted" fluted point, similar to the early Cumberland type from the eastern United States, provides an almost ideal connecting link between North and South America. Such specimens are few throughout Mexico and Central America, and they are all surface finds. Yet they are sufficiently distinctive to indicate that the Pleistocene projectile point horizon is represented in the important stretch that links the two continents of the New World.

In the Valley of Mexico, during the Pleistocene, sediments accumulated in shallow lakes, now dry. A particular zone of silts known as the Upper Becerra dates to this time. Most of the archaeological discoveries so far located in it probably date to 7000 B.C.

or 8000 B.C., to a time when the lakes were receding and exposed land was able to support now-extinct animals.

Before the Pleistocene Projectile Point Horizon

But at Tequixquiac a unique find from the base of the Upper Becerra may date back to 10000 B.C. or even to three or four thousand years earlier. A crude carving made of a camelid sacrum (see Figure 1.1) was intended to represent the head of an animal, perhaps a coyote. From the same fossiliferous stratum at Tequixquiac, some stone implements also are reported, including a miniature hand axe, but they are too few to provide any accurate notion of the nature of the total assemblage.

At Hueyatlaco in the Valsequillo reservoir of Puebla, Mexico, artifacts have been located in deeply stratified deposits with remains of mammoth, mastodon, camelid, wild horse, and four-horned antelope. In the earliest levels are flakes retouched along the edges to produce scrapers and possibly uniface projectile points. Some are associated with a mastodon kill. These simple tools continue into later horizons when crude blades became more common. Near the top of the deposits, well-made bifaces appear. One bi-point was found with bones of a horse. A stemmed point from the zone immediately above characterizes the last of the preceramic occupations.

Geologists do not consider a date of more than 18000 B.C. extreme, and a radiocarbon determination for an unspecified part of the Valsequillo sequence is 19900 B.C. ± 850. The fact that Pleistocene animals seem to have been thriving then, as well as later (they were found in the strata above), also supports the case for great age. By about 8000 B.C. in the nearby valley of Tehuacán, few now-extinct animals survived. Unfortunately, as at Valsequillo, the artifact samples are too small to give a clear idea of the total range of the assemblage.

In Tamaulipas in northeastern Mexico, the Diablo complex has been attributed an age in excess of 10000 B.C. One horse bone was found with a small series of roughly chipped tools including ovate bifaces, choppers, and scrapers. As at Hueyatlaco, man's ability to thin and flatten chipped stone artifacts is demonstrated, but

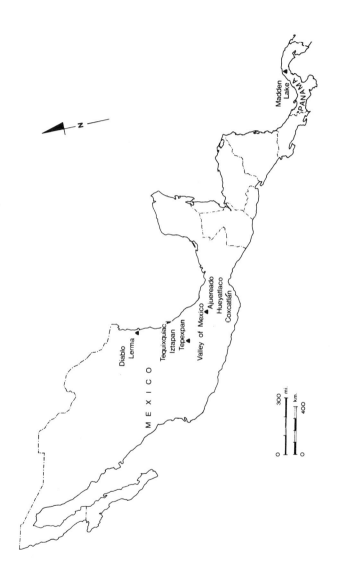

MAP 1.2   Early man sites in Mexico and Central America.

again the diagnostic specimens that could serve to link Diablo to other cultural complexes are absent.

After the Pleistocene Projectile Point Horizon

Following the Pleistocene projectile point horizon in Mexico and Central America, man appears to have played a diminishing role as a hunter. But near the village of Santa Isabel Iztapan, imperial mammoth bones from the Upper Becerra formation have been found alongside projectile points that would be considered of post-glacial age in North America. This species of mammoth apparently eluded hunters in both North and South America; possibly it was physically suited to survive longer in the Valley of Mexico.

"Tepexpan man" from a site nearby was apparently enclosed in Upper Becerra sediments at about the same time as Iztapan, probably 7000 B.C. to 8000 B.C. It is the skeleton, not of a man, but of a woman no more than thirty years of age. It differs in no significant measurements from many modern Mexicans. For this reason as much as any other, questions concerning its excavation have been raised. They remain unresolved, but the position of the skeleton within the Becerra deposits is lent credibility by fluorine tests, which show the human bones to be contemporaneous with extinct animals in the same formation.

North in Tamaulipas and southeast in Puebla two cultural phases, Lerma and Ajuereado, may have overlapped in time with Iztapan and Tepexpan. They are dated to approximately the same time, and they share similar choppers and crude scrapers. Wild plant foods were probably important, but hunting still provided much food. In early Ajuereado horses were rarely available. Hunters appear to have taken antelope and a Late Pleistocene species of jack rabbit in communal drives. Somewhat later, deer and cottontails, thought not to be so easily captured in drives, largely replaced other game animals. Relatively large hunting groups employing communal drives, then, may have been supplanted by smaller groups making intensive use of more restricted territories. In any event, it seems that the foundations for the Desert Culture were laid by 7000 B.C. The ever increasing emphasis on plant collecting prepared the indigenous peoples of Mexico for incipient horticulture, which was practiced in the Coxcatlán phase by 5000 B.C. Cultigens were to become ever more dominant in the diet.

Coincidentally, it seems to have been about 5000 B.C. that men first settled in the West Indies—in part as hunters, in part as collectors—from somewhere along the shores of Central America.

· SUMMARY AND SPECULATIONS

The conclusion that the first inhabitants of the Americas were primarily hunters of land mammals seems inescapable. During the Wisconsin glaciation the Bering-Chukchi region supported tundra and grasses that were suited to grazing animals, though virtually useless as a direct source of subsistence to man. Thus the High Arctic served as a filter, promoting free passage of hunters from Asia and inhibiting the passage of gatherers of plant foods. Nothing precludes the probability that sea-mammal hunters and fishermen were among the first to cross from Siberia to Alaska. But so far there is no evidence of them on an appropriately early time level, probably because many of their sites have been submerged or eroded away.

Recent investigations suggest that man may have entered the Americas well before the Classical Wisconsin. Known sites of this antiquity furnish a very hazy notion of the nature of the culture, and many more of them, soundly dated, are badly needed before the character and content of early occupations can be clearly formulated into an orderly arrangement. But while the samples are pitifully small, it does seem clear that big-game hunting was given appreciable emphasis throughout the Americas. Native horses and camels were ubiquitous. In more northerly regions, mammoth, bison, and caribou were commonly killed; in southerly regions, *megatheridae* and mastodon.

The artifacts of the pre-projectile point stage throughout the New World appear to be heterogeneous. If indeed they are, then either man had by that time been present in the Americas long enough to allow for wide cultural differentiation, or the early migrants to the New World drew upon diverse Asian industries ranging in character from Lower Paleolithic to Upper Paleolithic.

Neither interpretation is totally satisfying. The first demands acceptance of tremendous gaps in the archaeological record. The second makes it necessary to assume roughly contemporaneous but widely divergent Asiatic sources coexisting cheek by jowl, some of which would appear to have been badly fitted for the passage across hundreds of miles of the barren Arctic.

With the Pleistocene projectile point horizon, the Paleoamericans come into somewhat sharper focus. Though conceivably derived from the pre-projectile point stage, the pattern of life is strongly reminiscent of the Eurasian Upper Paleolithic, even to the point that nearly identical game animals were hunted, probably with communal drive techniques. Projectile points spread south to Tierra del Fuego by 9000 B.C., so rapidly as to suggest that their makers filled a cultural vacuum. Whether the culture was carried through the Americas by invaders or whether it diffused and was absorbed by indigenous populations is a question for future elucidation.

At the end of the Pleistocene projectile point horizon, many big game animals disappeared from the scene. Arguments have been launched to suggest that man was decisive in the Pleistocene extinctions. If he was, then his predatory attacks were no doubt most effective against such prime targets as slow-breeding mammoths, mastodons, and *megatheridae*. Even so, it is strange that horses should also vanish from the hemisphere, only to be introduced with renewed vigor by the Spaniards in historic times, especially considering the success of camelids in surviving in South America.

In the succeeding period glaciers had receded sufficiently for modern climatic and vegetation zones to begin to take shape. Man was obliged to face changed circumstances. Hunting remained a prominent occupation in many regions until about 6000 B.C. Some Pleistocene animals survived later locally, but it was essentially to modern fauna of moderate size that man turned: in Mexico to deer, and in South America to deer and camelids, particularly guanaco and llama. Small game and vegetal foods became progressively more basic to subsistence, and man learned to exploit these resources, seasonally and in local districts. Groups in arid regions soon came to rely almost entirely on plants for food and, in this dependence, eventually came to cultivate them. The high Mexican

plateaus provided all the necessary cultural and geographical conditions for plant domestication. New and different crops were
developed later in the Andean valleys. From these nuclei, food
producers were ultimately to spread widely and to lay secure foundations for native American culture growth.

· BIBLIOGRAPHIC ESSAY

More literature has been published on early man in North America
than on early man in Middle or South America, where the subject has
evidently been subordinated to that of archaeological high cultures. In
the following selections are general treatments giving wide coverage
and extensive bibliographies; they offer interpretations that may be
radically different from the one presented above.

In *Paleo-American Prehistory,* Occasional Papers of the Idaho State
University Museum, No. 16 (1965), A. L. Bryan's thesis is that man
reached Alaska during the Middle or Late Pleistocene. With his simple
tool kit, he then spread south. Laurel-leaf points, resembling hand-
axes, later diffused from Asia and were developed into projectile points.
In the appendix of the publication are useful synopses of New World
early man sites.

Alex D. Krieger, in defining the pre-projectile point stage in his
article, "Early Man in the New World," in J. D. Jennings and Edward
Norbeck, eds., *Prehistoric Man in the New World* (Chicago: University of Chicago Press, 1964), states that man may have arrived
in the Americas 35,000 to 40,000 years ago. The discussion in this
article ends with the emergence of the Archaic.

The existence of seven lithic technological traditions, some of which
are thought to have been imported during the Late Pleistocene from
Asia, others of which are considered indigenous developments, is
postulated by Edward Lanning in "Pleistocene Man in South America,"
World Archaeology, Vol. 2, No. 1 (1970), pp. 90–111.

T. F. Lynch speculates that men of the pre-projectile point stage
were largely supplanted by specialized big-game hunters, who in turn
were replaced by transhumant hunters and gatherers, some of them
eventually settling into local environmental niches and accepting farming. See his article *The Nature of the Central Andean Preceramic,* Oc-

casional Papers of the Idaho State University Museum, No. 21 (1967).

H. M. Wormington's book *Ancient Man in America*, 4th ed., Denver Museum of Natural History, Popular Series No. 4 (1957), is generally regarded as the standard reference, though now somewhat dated. It contains succinct summaries and interpretations of several important localities in North and Middle America.

In addition, the journal *American Antiquity* provides basic facts and speculation on early man. *Radiocarbon,* published by the American Journal of Science, not only lists dates but often gives capsule summaries of sites.

2
MESOAMERICA
PAUL TOLSTOY

· THE SETTING

In 1943 Paul Kirchhoff coined the term "Mesoamerica" for a part of the New World that, when the Europeans arrived, contained a distinctive civilization. For this civilization he listed some ninety-odd characteristics, ranging from a kind of digging stick called *coa* to hieroglyphic writing and from sandals with heels to step pyramids. The concept of Mesoamerica is, therefore, basically cultural in intent. It is, however, also a unit of geographic space and creates a field of inquiry that necessarily includes those cultures that existed in Mesoamerica prior to the rise of Mesoamerican civilization itself. As a unit of space (see Map 2.1), Mesoamerica includes a large part of what is today Mexico, as well as a substantial portion of Central America (Guatemala, Belize, El Salvador, and parts of Honduras, Nicaragua, and Costa Rica).

Physically, its outstanding characteristic is often thought to be its diversity, which results in contrasting environments existing within relatively short distances of one another. As a number of authors have suggested, this may have been a major factor shaping the rise of Mesoamerican civilization, inasmuch as it prompted individual human groups to exploit simultaneously more than one natural setting and to maintain exchange relationships with groups residing in environments differently endowed.

Two environmental characteristics were highly variable in Mesoamerica and, at the same time, crucial to man, according to William

29

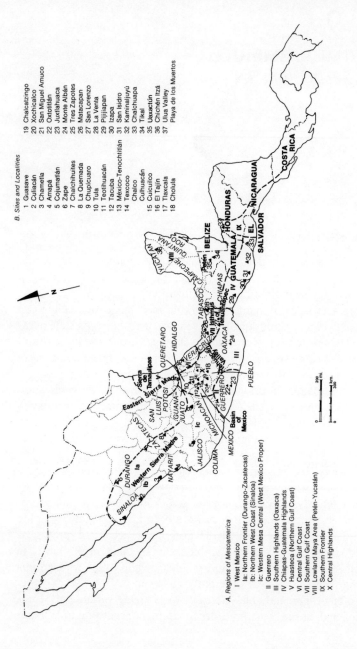

B. Sites and Localities

1 Guasave	19 Chalcatzingo
2 Culiacán	20 Xochicalco
3 Chametla	21 San Miguel Amuco
4 Amapá	22 Oxtotitlán
5 Cojumatlán	23 Juxtlahuaca
6 Zape	24 Monte Albán
7 Chalchihuites	25 Tres Zapotes
8 La Quemada	26 Matacapan
9 Chupícuaro	27 San Lorenzo
10 Tula	28 La Venta
11 Teotihuacán	29 Pijijiapan
12 Tacuba	30 Izapa
13 México-Tenochtitlán	31 San Isidro
14 Texcoco	32 Kaminaljuyú
Chalco	33 Chalchuapa
Culhuacán	34 Tikal
15 Cuicuilco	35 Uaxactún
16 El Tajín	36 Chichén Itzá
17 Tlaxcala	37 Ulúa Valley
18 Cholula	Playa de los Muertos

A. Regions of Mesoamerica

I West Mexico
  Ia: Northern Frontier (Durango-Zacatecas)
  Ib: Northern West Coast (Sinaloa)
  Ic: Western Mesa Central (West Mexico Proper)
II Guerrero
III Southern Highlands (Oaxaca)
IV Chiapas-Guatemala Highlands
V Huasteca (Northern Gulf Coast)
VI Central Gulf Coast
VII Southern Gulf Coast
VIII Lowland Maya Area (Petén-Yucatán)
IX Southern Frontier
X Central Highlands

MAP 2.1   Archaeological sites in Mesoamerica.

Sanders and Barbara Price: altitude and the availability of water. Most of Mesoamerica is highlands and lies above 1,000 meters of elevation. It presents a spectacular landscape of jagged mountains, steep-sided valleys, and inland basins. Much of this terrain is, in fact, above 2,000 meters, where the growing season for maize shrinks to seven or even six months. The highlands, on the whole, are dry, particularly west of the Isthmus of Tehuantepec. This limits the productivity of rainfall farming and means that irrigation, at times indispensable, is always rewarding.

Lowlands in Mesoamerica are less extensive. They are hotter and rainier than the highlands, this being particularly true of the Gulf coastal plain. At their worst, the lowlands offer easily leached soils, which, when farmed by the techniques of slash-and-burn, condition dispersed or shifting settlement. At their best, they allow as many as four crops of maize annually and provide a large number of useful wild plant and animal species.

Chart 2.1 shows the time periods and locations of various Mesoamerican cultures. In the early periods, human communities in Mesoamerica developed and applied the techniques needed to survive in the many environments at hand, first by hunting and gathering, then by farming. At a later stage, the adaptation of man to the setting of Mesoamerica transcended simple survival and became an attempt to pool these environments and their resources to sustain a single society. It is that attempt that we recognize as Mesoamerican civilization.

· FOOD COLLECTORS AND THE BEGINNINGS
OF AGRICULTURE (TO C. 2000 B.C.)

We still know little about the cultures that preceded village life and effective farming in Mesoamerica. Most of our knowledge comes from the Tehuacán Valley, a small arid depression on the eastern edge of the Southern Highlands of Mexico, and from two small regions near the eastern edge of Mesoamerica's northern frontier, the Sierra de Tamaulipas and the eastern Sierra Madre, both within the present state of Tamaulipas. These localities provide, not only more or less continuous sequences from Pleistocene times onward, but also conditions of preservation in dry caves that allow the

		SINALOA	DURANGO-ZACATECAS	WEST MEXICO	GUERRERO	CENTRAL HIGHLANDS	NORTHERN GULF
AZTEC HORIZON	1500	La Quinta	Loma San Gabriel	Periquillo	Tlam	Aztec	Panuco
	1400	Yebalito / El Taste					
	1300		Calera				(VI)
	1200	La Divisa					
	1100	Acaponeta	Río Tunal				Las Flores
	1000			Armeria			(V)
	900	Lolandis	Las Joyas / Retoño		Ita	Tula-Mazapan	Zaquil
	800			Colima			(IV)
	700	Baluarte	Ayala / Calichal				
TEOTIHUACAN HORIZON	600	Tierra del Padre	Loma San Gabriel / Alta Vista		Yax	Teotihuacán	Pithaya (III)
	500						
	400						
	300		Canutillo	Chupicuaro	Fal		El Prisco
	200 A.D.						(II)
	100					Patlachique	
	1			Ortices-Chanchopa		Ticoman	Chila (I)
	B.C. 200				Et		
	400		Los Caracoles		Rin	Zacatenco	Aguilar
	600				Tom		
	800					Tlatilco Style	Ponce
OLMEC HORIZON	1000			Capacha?	Uala	Ixtapaluca	Pavon
						Tlalpan?	Almagre
	2000				Pox		
					Ostiones		La Perra
	3000					San Nicolas	
	4000						Nogales
						Tecolote	
	5000						
	6000					Hidalgo	
	7000						Lerma
						San Juan	
	8000						
						Hueyatlaco	Diablo?
						El Horno?	

CHART 2.1   Phases of Mesoamerican culture.

CENTRAL GULF	SOUTHERN HIGHLANDS	SOUTHERN GULF	ISTHMUS		PETEN	GUATEMALA HIGHLANDS	HONDURAS
Isla de Sacrificios 2-3	Late Salada / Albán 5	Cerro de las Mesas 4	(Chinautla Polychrome)	Urbina (XII) / Tuxtla	New Town	Chinautla	(Post-Plumbate)
	4			Suchiapa (XI-B)			
Isla de Sacrificios 1	Early Venta	Soncuatla	(Tohil Plumbate)	Ruiz (XI-A)		Amatle 3	(Tohil Plumbate)
Remojadas Superior 2 (El Tajín)	3B	Tres Zapotes 4		Marcos / Paredon (X-B)	Tepeu	Amatle 2	Ulua-Yojoa Polychrome
				Maravillas (X-A)			
Remojadas Superior 1	Late Palo Blanco 3A	Cerro de Las Mesas 3	(Tiquisate Ware)	Laguna (IX)		Esperanza	
	2/3A			Jiquipilas (VIII)	Tzakol	Aurora	Usulutan-Bichrome
Remojadas Inferior	Early 2	Las Mesas 2	Tiestal	Istmo (VII)	Floral Park	Verbena-Arenal	
	Late Santa María / Monte 1	Tres Zapotes 1	Izapa-Crucero	Horcones (VI)	Chicanel		
El Trapiche 3			Con-chas 2	Guanacaste (V)		Providencia-Sacate Pequez	
	Early Santa María / Guadalupe	Palangana	1	La Francesa (IV) / Escalera (III)	Mamom		
El Trapiche 2	San José	Nacaste (La Venta)	Jocotal	Dili (II)	Xe	Las Charcas	
		San Lorenzo	Cuadros	Cotorra (I)		Arevalo	
El Trapiche 1	Ajalpan	Chicharras	Ocós				Yarumela 1?
		Bajío / Ojochi	Barra				
	Purrón						
	Abejas						
Palma Sola?			Islona de Chantuto?				
	Coxcatlán						
	El Riego					El Chayal?	
	Ajuereado						

recovery of plant remains. A number of other sites, most of them in the highlands, have yielded supplementary evidence that can be understood in the light of the Tehuacán and Tamaulipas remains.

In the Tehuacán sequence, four phases are recognized prior to the appearance of pottery c. 2000 B.C. in C_{14} years. These are: (1) Ajuereado (?8500–7000 B.C.), in which hunting is estimated to have accounted for most of the diet (by volume); (2) El Riego (7000–5000 B.C.), in which meat and vegetal food were consumed in about equal amounts and a small proportion (5 percent) of the latter was apparently grown; (3) Coxcatlán (5000–3300 B.C.); and (4) Abejas (3300–2000 B.C.), in which hunting provided about 30 percent of the food intake, vegetal food accounting for the rest. In the latter two phases, food from cultivated plants rose from 14 percent to 21 percent of the total diet. These gross trends are paralleled in the Sierra Madre sequence of Tamaulipas. Changes also took place in species used, in the manner of their procurement, and in the manner of their processing for food.

The Ajuereado phase is, strictly speaking, beyond the range of our present concern. It should nevertheless be noted that an important shift occurs within that phase—namely, from the hunting of gregarious animals (horse, antelope, jackrabbit) to that of more solitary species (deer, cottontail), with a consequent reduction in size of the hunting group itself. Though the Early Ajuereado bands may not have been the singleminded "big-game hunters" of some reconstructions, it seems evident that the shift to Late Ajuereado just described is a local echo of such transitions as that from Paleolithic to Mesolithic in temperate Europe, and that from Lithic to Archaic postulated by Gordon Willey and Philip Phillips for the Western Hemisphere as a whole.

By far the most interesting fact about the phases that follow is the consumption of cultivated plants in increasing amounts. Four species give evidence of cultivation in El Riego times: chili pepper, avocado, amaranth, and squash (*Cucurbita mixta*). Of these, amaranth, a grain plant, and avocado are known to have wild antecedents locally. In the Coxcatlán phase, seven more species are evidence of cultivation: a squash (*C. moschata*), the bottle gourd, three fruits (*chupandilla,* white *zapote,* and black *zapote*), the common bean, and, most important of all, maize. All except maize and *chupandilla* are considered intruders into the Tehuacán Valley. It is significant that the order of appearance of new species in Tamaulipas differs from that in the Tehuacán Valley. Thus, though chili occurs in both sequences from the start, the bottle gourd and the pumpkin (*C. pepo*) are earlier in Tamaulipas and the common bean is perhaps slightly earlier, whereas maize and amaranth are definitely later. This evidence, and the number of plants found in the Tehuacán sequence that were apparently domesticated elsewhere, indicate that plant domestication was proceeding in many regions of Mesoamerica and that in each region from 7000 B.C. onward it involved different local plants. These evidently then spread more or less rapidly as domesticates to regions where they were not native. Whether this process deserves to be called one of "multiple origins" or whether it is the complex aftermath of some more remote "single origin" of farming in Mesoamerica remains an open question, if not one that is often acknowledged.

By 3500 B.C. the staples of the Mesoamerican diet (maize, beans, squash, chili peppers) were being grown in Tehuacán and probably elsewhere. Abejas sees the improvement of domesticated maize (some of it due to hybridization with varieties and relatives from outside Tehuacán). When prepared for consumption, this corn was soaked with lime and ground into a fine flour (today known as *nixtamal*) on a longish flat slab (*metate*) by means of an oblong handstone (*mano*) held in both hands. This procedure and these utensils are, to this day, basic to Mesoamerican cookery.

If the tools and weapons from other sites of this period are any guide, we may conclude that by 5000 B.C. many communities of highland Mexico shared in a fairly homogeneous pattern, which Richard S. MacNeish calls the Tehuacán tradition. This is indicated by materials from sites in Chiapas, Oaxaca, the Basin of Mexico, Hidalgo, and Querétaro. The Tamaulipas materials, however, seem divergent in several ways and suggest a related but separate tradition. Similarly, the contemporary Cochise phases of the North American Southwest, and probably nonfarming Big Bend communities of Mexico's northern plateau must represent equally distinct traditions, perhaps sharing a common "Desert Culture" background at the pre-5000 B.C. level but recognizably different thereafter. Thus, site distributions suggest that, in the highlands at least, a boundary was emerging that prefigured the one that was later to separate Mesoamerica from neighboring areas to the north.

Though the diet, the tool kit, and even, in part, the geographic distribution of the Tehuacán tradition anticipate later conditions, it is still too early to speak of the emergence of Mesoamerican culture. For one thing, the social, political, and religious super-structures of Mesoamerican life are still missing. In fact, the threshold of sedentary life itself may have been barely attained in Abejas times. Mostly, the Coxcatlán and Abejas people came together in village-like communities during the rainy season to tend their crop, only to break up and wander in search of wild foods during the dry winter. Admittedly, the pull toward sedentism was there and growing as reliance on food crops increased. But the trend was a slow one, and a full 5,000 years intervened between the acquisition of farming techniques and dependence upon them to the extent of year-round stable residence. And until stable villages existed, many essential features of Mesoamerican civilization were precluded.

Also, Tehuacán tradition sites appear to be absent from the lowlands. This could be for lack of investigation, for sites earlier than 2000 B.C. are still virtually unknown outside of the highlands. There are hints, however, that the lowlands at this time harbored a way of life altogether different, one essentially distinct in its subsistence basis and its tool kit and perhaps well ahead of Tehuacán in the stability of its residence pattern. It would seem, therefore, that one major feature of the later Mesoamerican pattern was still missing—namely, the participation of the lowlands in a way of life common to the entire area.

In attempting to explain the switch to farming as the basis of subsistence, we must answer two questions: (1) What impelled particular communities increasingly to neglect wild food in favor of domesticates? And (2) how did the technique of plant cultivation come into being?

To the first question, Kent Flannery in 1968 provided an elegant answer. He pointed out that the genetic plasticity of such plants as wild maize made them respond to cultivation by increasing yield. Increased yield will sustain a larger and less mobile population, which in turn will practice cultivation on an increased scale and, it might be added, may eventually need to do so to sustain itself. Therefore, once initiated, the cultivation of certain species is a process that, unlike wild food procurement, amplifies itself at the expense of other subsistence practices.

To the second question, a convincing answer must take into account that several groups of food collectors devised the technique in end-Pleistocene times, that none apparently did so earlier, and that some never acquired it. Perhaps, as some have suggested, the main requirement is simply a degree of intensity in the interaction between human and plant communities and the presence of suitable species in the latter. Perhaps the early post-Pleistocene was the first time in the history of human societies when relative population pressure, the efficiency of hunting, and the extinction of certain animal species could combine to make hunting counterproductive in certain areas and to direct human groups in those areas toward a particularly intense use of plant foods. The chances would then have risen that such factors as food preparation and disposal habits, site preference patterns, a repetitive annual migration cycle, and the availability of suitable species would join to create situations in which cultivation would appear. Concretely, some human groups could have found themselves annually harvesting a crop that they themselves had earlier, and inadvertently, sown. Since the "sowing" would consist of the abandonment of seeds or cuttings (whether in the process of preparation or waste disposal) of plants originally collected for food, we can assume that the crop would, from the start, incur the pressure of artificial selection. With a responsive organism such as maize, this would be enough to trigger the self-amplifying mechanism outlined by Flannery. How many times this process may have repeated itself depends, of course, on the probability of its occurrence, which has yet to be estimated. It also depends on the speed with which the technique spread from the center or centers of its initial appearance, thereby precluding its independent appearance in the areas into which it diffused.

· EARLY VILLAGERS (2000–1200 B.C.)

Settled village life and pottery (Figure 2.1) are thought to appear at about the same time in Mesoamerica and to mark the beginning of

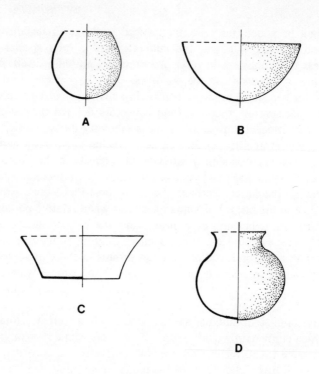

FIGURE 2.1   Earliest basic shapes of Mesoamerican pottery.   *(A) Tecomate.*   *(B)* Simple hemispherical bowl.   *(C)* Flat-based pan or dish.   *(D) Olla.*

the Formative or Preclassic. The Tehuacán sequence has pottery first appearing in the Purrón phase, probably between 2300 and 2000 B.C. Comparably ancient pottery is found on the Pacific coast of Guerrero, in deep deposits of the Pox phase at the sites of Puerto Marquez and Zanja. Solid evidence of sedentary life is lacking in either instance, however, and we can only interpolate, at least in Tehuacán, from the fact that small but fully sedentary communities are known in the next phase, called Ajalpan, and may possibly have existed at the end of the preceding one, Abejas.

Pottery is earlier in Ecuador and Colombia and is equally old at the site of Monagrillo in Panama. Yet, neither the shapes of Purrón and Pox pottery (a globular, restricted-mouth jar, or *teco-*

mate, in both phases; a flat-based pan and a necked jar, or *olla,* in Purrón) nor its rudimentary decoration (an occasional incised line in Pox) show particularly convincing parallels to early South American wares. It is commonly concluded that this is a case of stimulus diffusion, in which the technique of firing clay to make containers was borrowed, but without the kind of direct or intense exposure to South American sources (or at least to those presently known) to bring about close copies of foreign originals.

Our knowledge of the millennium that follows is still very spotty, though for the first time we get a glimpse of developments in the lowlands. A number of sites on both sides of the Isthmus of Tehuantepec reveal a tradition of elaborate, well-made pottery in existence between 1600 and 1200 B.C. This tradition's immediate antecedents are obscure. Phases so far recognized include Barra (?1600–1300 B.C.) and Ocós (1300–1200 B.C.) on the Pacific side in Chiapas and adjacent Guatemala, Ojochi (?1450–1350 B.C.) and Bajío (1350–1250 B.C.) in southern Veracruz. The *tecomate* and flat-based dish forms in this pottery suggest links with the highlands, but a variety of stamping and incision techniques used for decoration are new. Some, such as criss-cross incision, brushing, fingernail impressing, rocker-stamping and shell-stamping suggest the earlier Valdívia pottery of coastal Ecuador. Others occur in the contemporary or later pottery of Machalilla, which is also in coastal Ecuador. Finally, still others (e.g., cord-marking), found only in the Ocós phase, are so far unique in the New World at this early time level and might indicate contacts with eastern Asia. More generally, this pottery, and most particularly that of Ocós, is suggestive of sea-borne contacts with remote regions within the Pacific basin, and of a maritime orientation of some coastal communities at this time.

In the highlands, known materials of comparable age include those of the Early Ajalpan phase in Tehuacán, the Tierras Largas phase in Oaxaca, and, possibly, the Tlalpan phase in the Basin of Mexico. Generally, highland ceramics seem simpler than those of the lowlands in their repertory of shapes and decorations. Red-on-brown painting, destined to have a long history in Mesoamerica, occurs both in Tehuacán and in Oaxaca. Small permanent villages occur in both these valleys, and there is, in fact, every reason to believe that similar communities existed at this time through most of Mesoamerica.

As suggested earlier, such villages in the highlands probably arose as an adjunct to dependence on maize, beans, and squash. The Tehuacán sequence, moreover, shows that maize was constantly improving its characteristics as a food plant as a result of selection, of crossing with other varieties, and of hybridization with wild relatives called *Tripsacum* and *Zea mexicana* (*teosinte*). In the lowlands, however, the basis of village life could have been different. Not only could abundant and localized resources have supported village life without farming in some regions, as Michael Coe and Kent Flannery have pointed out, but the earliest cultivation to appear may have been that of root crops, as Gareth Lowe has suggested. The absence of *manos* and *metates* at sites of the Pacific plain phases and the prevalence of obsidian chips suited for insertion into manioc graters have been cited as evidence to this effect. However, pollen evidence from Guatemala and Panama indicates that, as early as 2000 B.C., maize was grown in Central America, though, of course, we do not know how important it may have been as a food.

· THE OLMEC HORIZON (1200–900 B.C.)

By far the most spectacular event of the second millennium B.C. in the New World is the appearance of Olmec culture in the lowlands of southern Veracruz. Perhaps some or many features of Olmec culture will be found to occur earlier elsewhere in Mesoamerica or outside it. Present evidence, however, indicates that an unrivaled degree of cultural complexity was achieved at the site of San Lorenzo in southern Veracruz. About 1200 B.C. on the radiocarbon time-scale, the Southern Lowlands of the Gulf coast provide evidence of massed economic power, of what appears to be a socially stratified society, and of the related phenomena of civilized life.

The carving of stone monuments at San Lorenzo apparently begins in the Chicharras phase (1250–1150 B.C.). In the San Lorenzo phase that follows, hundreds of stone monuments are in place on a huge platform built by heaping thousands of tons of fill around a natural eminence. These monuments are mostly sculptures in the round, made of basalt quarried some 70 kilometers away, and include eight giant heads, weighing many tons, carved to portray individuals whom we can only guess to be members of a ruling dynasty (Figure 2.2). Similar heads and monuments occur at the site of La Venta, some 85 kilometers away, in Tabasco. La Venta may have been occupied contemporaneously with San Lorenzo and for some centuries after. Finds at La Venta not duplicated at San Lorenzo include human figures and other items made of jade. These mark the beginning of an enduring pattern in Mesoamerica, the appreciation of jade as a substance of value and as an important element in art and ceremonialism.

The Olmecs (named, incorrectly, after the historical inhabitants of the southern Gulf coast) occupy two key positions in the history of Mesoamerica: that of purveyors over a broad area of many, if not most, of the features that make for the cultural unity of Mesoamerica from then onward; and that of the earliest example in the New World of a stage in cultural evolution called "civilization."

The role of the Olmecs as the original unifiers of Mesoamerica is suggested by the distribution of Olmec-related materials. Pottery closely similar to that of San Lorenzo serves to define a series of contemporaneous phases in coastal Chiapas (Cuadros), highland Chiapas (Cotorra), Oaxaca (San José), central Veracruz (El Trapiche), southern Puebla (Late Ajalpan), Morelos (La Juana), the Basin of Mexico (Ixtapaluca), and perhaps parts of Guerrero. Ceramic features found in almost all these phases include flat-based dishes with incised and carved designs in Olmec style, rocker stamping, differentially fired ware and baby-faced figures, large and small. Monuments carved in Olmec style occur in El Salvador (Chalchuapa), Chiapas (San Isidro, Pijijiapan), Morelos (Chalcatzingo), and Guerrero (San Miguel Amuco). To these may be added the cave paintings of Oxtotitlán and Juxtlahuaca, also in Guerrero. These materials (unlike the even more widespread portable objects in Olmec style, which may have been distributed by trade) necessarily imply the presence over most of Mesoamerica of people who shared the ritual and the beliefs of the builders of San Lorenzo and La Venta. Significantly, this evidence is present in lowlands and highlands alike, suggesting that, for the first time,

FIGURE 2.2   Giant Olmec head from San Lorenzo, San Lorenzo
phase (1150–950 B.C.).

these two zones were being exploited by a single sociocultural organism. This may also be the meaning of the spread at this time into the lowlands of such highland features as the manufacture of obsidian blades and ground stone celts and adzes.

We may never know the full range of intangible culture elements spread by the Olmecs. The occurrence in Olmec art of many elements that have known meanings in later traditions make it very likely, however, that the Olmecs introduced, wherever they went, many of the deities, myths, rituals, and calendrical concepts found later among such peoples as the Mayas, Zapotecs, Mixtecs, and Aztecs. There are even hints of a writing system, though the evidence for it is still scant.

It has been argued that the Olmecs had not acceded to the status of civilization, a stage that implies, among other things, a "state" organization at the political level. An adequate discussion of this point would require both an examination of how civilization is to be defined and an evaluation of the relevant data on the Olmecs. Neither can be attempted here. We shall be content to note that if we grant the Olmecs full-time sculptors and engineers and a calendrical system, it is likely that they also satisfied most of the other criteria of civilization proposed by various authors.

Both the causes behind the rise of the Olmecs and the nature of their dominance over much of Mesoamerica are still obscure. Engineering and other activities at San Lorenzo imply a large supportive population, and a correspondingly sufficient food supply. To account for the latter, MacNeish has suggested the impact of highland farming (perhaps a high-yielding variety of maize) on a previously sedentary, well-fed population. It still has to be shown how civilization would constitute a response to this economic change. The answer may lie, as Coe and Sanders have implied, in the possibilities that arise for the unequal access of groups or individuals to the new wealth, perhaps the latter being in the form of productive land or of the key crop itself.

Once set in motion, the interaction of expanding food supply, growing population, and deepening social cleavages is probably a self-intensifying process. Its limits are all the harder to predict as they are often set, not by the productivity of the society in which the process begins, but by the ability of that society to exploit its neighbors. In a general way, it is this ability that we are measuring as we plot the distribution of Olmec remains over Mesoamerica. More concretely, of course, Olmec "imperialism"—in itself a criterion of civilized status—may have taken a variety of forms, from the creation of satellites among suppliers of magnetite and ilmenite in the valley of Oaxaca, as Flannery has suggested, to outright homesteading in the lowlands of Tabasco or Chiapas, or to expeditionary activities in Guerrero or in the Basin of Mexico. The precise events and processes behind Olmec "influence" are still far from established. What does seem likely is that the Olmecs were the first society to benefit fully from the potential of highland farming in the lowlands. Having created a society viable in both zones and one expansionistic by nature, the Olmecs went on through a variety of interactions to stimulate other societies to recast themselves in a similar mold and to become part of a new maximal society, the first to be truly Mesoamerican.

· TLATILCO—WEST MEXICO IN THE PRECLASSIC

An enigmatic style, variously labeled "Tlatilco," "Amacuzac," and "Río Cuautla," is represented by the contents of several hundred graves uncovered since 1941 at Tlatilco, on the western edge of Mexico City, and at a number of sites in Morelos and Guerrero. At Tlatilco itself, such graves may be somewhat younger (1000–900 B.C.?) than others containing typical Olmec (Ixtapaluca) pottery, though some contact and fusion of the two traditions is suggested. Features shared by Tlatilco with some of the lowland pre-Olmec pottery earlier described, as well as certain recent finds in western Mexico, could mean that the style will be shown eventually to be older outside of the Central Highlands.

Though containing elements frequently found on the Olmec horizon, Tlatilco pottery is much more varied. *Ollas* with trumpet-like necks, cylindrical-neck bottles, waisted bottles (with hourglass- or spool-shaped bodies), stirrup spouts, effigies, kidney-shaped bowls, pedestal cups, square forms, tripods, tetrapods, handles, gadrooning, resist-painting, masks, and seals are among its distinctive features. This material is unequally distributed in the graves and suggests important status differences among the occupants.

The Tlatilco style exhibits intriguing and far-flung parallels, within Mesoamerica and outside it, that it is still difficult to account for with any precision. On and beyond the western margins of Mesoamerica, certain later styles such as that of Chupícuaro in Guanajuato (*c.* 300 B.C.–A.D. 1) and that of the Ortices phase and related shaft tombs of Colima, Jalisco, and Nayarit (*c.* 200 B.C.– A.D. 200?) share with Tlatilco a considerable number of highly specific presences and absences. Within Mesoamerica proper, features first found in Tlatilco eventually find their way into many later assemblages, though their trajectories appear erratic, unpredictable, with certain concentrated occurrences, as in Monte Albán I in Oaxaca and Playa de los Muertos in Honduras, that are, at present, unexplainable. Farther afield, specific similarities may be seen with roughly contemporaneous wares of the Andean area (e.g., certain bottle forms, stirrup spouts, and effigies) and even with some of the Lungshanoid pottery of south China and southeast Asia (e.g., tall tripods, tetrapods, pedestal cups, and square forms). Like the Ocós style of the Isthmus, Tlatilco hints at maritime contacts between western Mesoamerica and remote portions of the Pacific rim. Both the local and long-range connections of Tlatilco, however, require fuller sequences and better dating from a number of regions before their real meaning can be assessed.

· THE CONSOLIDATION OF MESOAMERICA: THE MIDDLE, LATE, AND TERMINAL PRECLASSIC (900 B.C.–A.D. 250)

We do not know why ceremonial activities cease at San Lorenzo *c.* 950 B.C., when the monuments are mutilated and buried in accordance with a deliberate plan. These events may reflect internal stresses within Olmec society or the intrusion of outsiders who, if not totally alien, must have been at least alienated. Shortly thereafter, Olmec influence over Mesoamerica loses its directness and intensity. A series of regional cultures take shape and engage in seemingly autonomous growth. At the same time, and despite the decentralization implicit in the decline of the Olmecs, there is no question that Mesoamerica retains its unity, continues to share and enlarge a pool of commonly held characteristics, and remains a network of mutually interdependent local societies.

To demonstrate this unity, it would be possible to list the many traits whose distribution throughout Mesoamerica probably date from the Olmec horizon and which are generally retained thereafter. They range from tools and food-preparation habits to religious concepts and patterns of trade and of status definition. It is also possible to show continuing contact among all parts of the Mesoamerican network by noting how, again and again, fashions in pottery-making and decoration became shared by regions as remote from one another as the Central Highlands and the Petén, or Honduras and Oaxaca. Here, however, we shall only outline briefly, region by region, the appearance of such characteristics (e.g., monumental art, architecture site planning, writing, dense populations, luxury crafts) as measure the growing capacity of particular regions and communities to support the superstructure of civilized life. Their appearance may also be viewed as the unfolding of trends initiated by the contact of local communities with Olmec civilization.

In southern Veracruz and Tabasco, Olmec ceremonialism at La Venta evidently survives by some three centuries the burial of the monuments at San Lorenzo. The period after the abandonment of La Venta c. 600 B.C. is poorly understood but is probably represented by the site of Tres Zapotes, with its reliefs in the style that has been called Izapan. In highland Chiapas, ceremonial building activity is thought to have occurred from Dili times (c. 800 B.C.) onward and grows in scale through the following Escalera (550–450 B.C.) and La Francesa (450–250 B.C.) phases. At Izapa, near the Guatemalan border, massive construction evidently begins in the Duende phase (c. 700–500 B.C.), contemporary of Dili and Escalera to the west. Izapa then becomes the largest ceremonial center on the Pacific side of Mesoamerica. The Izapan style of stone carving, named after the site and perpetuating numerous Olmec themes and conventions, extends geographically from Tres Zapotes through highland Chiapas and into highland Guatemala, where it is associated with Miraflores phase remains at the site of Kaminaljuyú. The Isthmian and highland Guatemalan regions, therefore, appear united culturally in the centuries before the beginning of our era and, at the same time, as direct heirs to the lowland Olmecs. At Kaminaljuyú, the famous tomb 2 of mound

E-III-3 of the Miraflores Arenal phase, with its offerings of jade, innumerable pottery vessels, and sacrificed adults and children, is evidence of a social order in which the privileged few were no less powerful than they had been at San Lorenzo or La Venta. Several sites with Izapa-style reliefs also contain monuments carved with dates in the so-called Long Count system (in which elapsed time is reckoned from a fixed initial point at 3113 B.C.), which we can read because its notation is that of the later Mayas, who adopted it. We may doubt that these dates represent the actual beginnings of writing or calendrics, though they are the earliest examples of stone monuments commemorating dated events. This trait and others, including the Izapan style itself, mark these cultures as the intermediaries in space and time that may have conveyed the basic elements of Mesoamerican civilization out of the original Olmec heartland into the Maya area.

The Lowland Maya region contains evidence of settlement by pottery-using farmers *c.* 900 B.C. From the initial ceramic phase in Guatemala, called Xe and known from a very few sites, through the local horizons known as Mamom and Chicanel, the density of settlement grows noticeably. Chicanel (*c.* 300 B.C.–A.D. 250) is marked by ceremonial and funerary architecture at such sites as Tikal and Uaxactún and shows clear evidence of participation in the Izapan style of the highlands to the south and west. There are linguistic arguments for considering these Lowland Mayas as descendants of groups who must have lived in or near the Olmec heartland prior to 1000 B.C. As pioneer settlers in a sparsely inhabited region, they may have brought with them the essentials of Mesoamerican civilization, which they translated into increasingly complex social arrangements, art, and architecture as they grew demographically and economically. A catalytic role in this process may have been played by continued contact with the highlands to the south.

On the other side of the Isthmus, in the Southern and Central Highlands, trends take place not unlike those just described, with one very important difference, which becomes accentuated with time. Whereas the regions so far dealt with perpetuate the Olmec pattern of residence in small villages or scattered homesteads, the highlanders west of the Isthmus come to inhabit increasingly large communities that eventually become true cities. This tendency may be related to the practice of irrigation, which becomes more and more essential in the highlands as population increases.

In highland Oaxaca, some communities of the Guadalupe phase (700–500 B.C.) cover a surface of 40 hectares. Residential areas twice this size appear in the following Monte Albán I phase (500–200 B.C.). By 500 B.C., Monte Albán itself—an architectural complex grandiosely set on the summit of a mountain overlooking the valley of Oaxaca—had been founded. The initial occupation at that site is notable for a distinctive, Olmec-related style of low-relief carving that depicts contorted and mutilated figures (the so-called *danzantes,* probably prisoners of war; see Figure 2.3). A writing system is in evidence and, though not fully legible, reveals the existence of the 260-day cycle of the Mesoamerican calendar. This cycle—a basic unit of time-reckoning in Mesoamerica—results from the permutation of the numerals 1 through 13 with 20 day-names, a given combination of number and day occurring only once in a cycle. The Monte Albán II phase, which follows (A.D. 1–200), is characterized by large sites, further building activity at Monte Albán itself, and inscriptions relating to the military conquests of the rulers of that site.

In the Central Highlands, the post-Olmec Zacatenco phase of the Basin of Mexico is known mainly from a number of small village sites and thus presents a distinctly rural aspect. However, work at Cuicuilco raises the possibility that several round ceremonial platforms were built at that site in Zacatenco times. A contemporary occupation at the site of Tlatilco covers some 60 hectares. In later phases (Ticoman, 500–50 B.C.; Patlachique, 50 B.C.–A.D. 1) Cuicuilco evidently becomes a large settlement with several pyramids, possibly a true city. The growth of Cuicuilco and the abundance of contemporary sites in other parts of the Basin of Mexico may be related to the practice, appearing now for the first time, of large-scale farming on the basin floor (earlier cultivation appears to have been mainly on hillsides), itself perhaps made profitable by irrigation and, conceivably, the draining of lakeshore swamps to create productive grids of gardens and canals called *chinampas,* still used today in the Basin of Mexico.

Cuicuilco, however, is soon eclipsed by Teotihuacán, a site in a

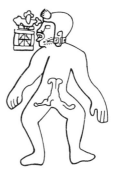

Based on illustrations in L. Séjourné, *El Universo de Quetzalcoatl* (Mexico City: Fondo de Cultura Económica, 1962).

FIGURE 2.3   Contorted figures *(danzantes)* carved in relief on stone slabs at Monte Albán, Oaxaca. Monte Albán I phase (500–200 B.C.).

northwestern extension of the Basin of Mexico formed by the valley of the Río San Juan. Between 50 B.C. and A.D. 1 in C_{14} years (probably 50 B.C. and A.D. 50 in calendar years), Teotihuacán consists of two large adjoining settlements, totaling some 400 hectares. A century later (in the Teotihuacán I, or Tzacualli, phase), these are fused into a single community covering some 1,700 hectares (17 square kilometers) and containing some 30,000 people. In Teotihuacán II, or Miccaotli, times (A.D. 150–200 calendar time), Teotihuacán sprawls over 22.5 square kilometers with some 45,000 inhabitants.

Teotihuacán probably depended on irrigation in growing its food supply. The need for this technique may have been particularly acute just prior to the growth of the city if we are to believe indications that rainfall at that time was scantier than it is today. What may have begun as a series of measures for the maintenance of the status quo evidently triggered demographic growth, which, for reasons still not fully understood, was accompanied by a concentration of population at Teotihuacán itself and an actual reduction in the number and size of rural communities. The result was a new era in which Teotihuacán became the single most powerful community in Mesoamerica and extended its influence accordingly.

· THE MAJOR TRADITIONS OF THE CLASSIC
(A.D. 250–900)

The beginning of the Classic is perhaps best thought of as a threshold beyond which most regions of Mesoamerica achieve a certain level of economic and cultural development. Differences of course remain in population density, settlement pattern, productivity, degree of social differentiation, and political power. Yet, even such underdeveloped regions as highland Chiapas or the valley of Tehuacán are now sufficiently wedded to the Mesoamerican system as a whole to sustain their own ceremonial centers, their own local élites, and their own full-time artisans and traders. Rather than being hinterlands for one or two remote centers, most regions of Mesoamerica now harbor subsystems that replicate the social order for which the Olmecs produced the template.

As a result, regions now relate to one another on more equal terms, and to the interdependence created over a millennium ago is now added competition. A more even distribution of power is manifest in cultural regionalization and the emergence of several coordinate traditions within Mesoamerica, of which the main ones are those of Teotihuacán, of El Tajín, of Monte Albán, and of the Lowland Maya region. Somewhat paradoxically, competition came to reinforce Mesoamerican unity whenever a particular tradition was successfully extended by its bearers beyond its home range.

The outstanding example of this, of course, is the spread of the Teotihuacán variant of Mesoamerican civilization. Teotihuacán pottery, including the famed cylindrical tripods with stucco or relief decoration, specific elements of iconography such as representations of Tlaloc (a raingod of ultimately Olmec derivation and probably the patron deity of Teotihuacán), and even features of architectural design spread by A.D. 300 or shortly thereafter into Guatemala (highland and lowland), the Isthmus, Veracruz, Oaxaca, and Guerrero. In archaeological terms, this is a clear-cut horizon style, the second one to exist in Mesoamerica. In historical terms, we may have here a conquest empire, as Ignacio Bernal and others have suggested.

The vastness of Teotihuacán *c.* A.D. 200 has been noted. In the phases called Tlalmimilolpa (A.D. 200–300) and Xolalpan (A.D. 300–600), the city continues to grow, not in area, but in population, which is estimated at about 85,000 in the second of these phases. The genuine urban nature of the site is apparent from its size and the impressiveness of its ceremonial core, disposed along a broad avenue 2½ kilometers in length and including the gigantic Pyramid of the Sun, 65 meters in height, as well as from the internal diversity of its residential zone. An example of the city's architecture is shown in Figure 2.4. Not only did certain kinds of craft specialists, such as obsidian workers, gravitate to particular quarters of the city, but some neighborhoods evidently housed outsiders from other parts of Mesoamerica, such as Oaxaca and the Maya region. A strong central authority is implied by the planning of the city, laid out in blocks that share a common orientation, and also by the distribution of surrounding rural communities, which seemingly reflects overall administrative policy rather than local needs. Murals, representations on pottery vessels, clay figurines,

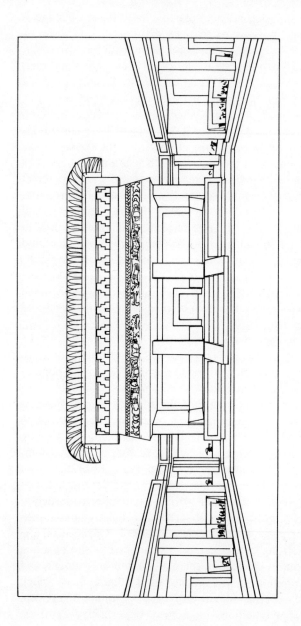

Based on an illustration in L. Séjourné, *Arquitectura y Pintura en Teo-tihuacán* (Mexico City: Siglo Veintiuno Editores, 1966).

FIGURE 2.4 A Teotihuacán temple, at a location called Zacuala within the urban zone of Teotihuacán. Xolalpan phase (A.D. 300–600).

and stone carvings, large and small, throw some light on the religious beliefs and practices that probably served to justify the power of city's rulers. These show specific parallels to those of Postclassic times, aside from their generic resemblance to those of Mesoamerica as a whole. Writing was evidently known, though it does not generally occur on monuments.

The real power of Teotihuacán and of its rulers was, without doubt, economic and probably stemmed, not only from the efficient management of local food and other resources, but from the control over the production and trade of luxuries (cacao, rubber, minerals) from distant parts of Mesoamerica, some of them (such as southern Veracruz and highland Guatemala) perhaps under the direct political control of the metropolis. We may surmise further that this control was, in some measure, achieved and protected by military means, as it was later by the Aztecs, whom we know better. But since this military control was weak at Teotihuacán, it seems to have failed in the Metepec phase, which represents a century of decline following the Xolalpan phase and ends with the burning of the city *c.* A.D. 700 or shortly thereafter.

As noted earlier, portions of the Gulf coast may have been under direct Teotihuacán domination in Classic times. This is most likely to be true of the old Olmec heartland of southern Veracruz, where the temple platform at Matacapan suggests the work of Teotihuacán architects, according to Coe. Direct domination may also have been the case in the Huasteca, though there strong Teotihuacán influence is evident mainly in pottery of the Pithaya (Panuco III) phase, as neither large sites nor stone monuments occur.

The central Gulf coast, however, is dominated by the so-called Tajín, or Classic Veracruz, style or tradition, whose major center was El Tajín, noted for its Pyramid of the Niches. Though the site appears to have been not a city but a typical lowland ceremonial center supported by peasants whose houses were scattered over the countryside, El Tajín was probably a major political force in its time, as suggested by the fact that it retained its cultural identity through the period of Teotihuacán dominance. Tajín ornamental art, somewhat reminiscent of the decoration found on Chinese bronzes of the Chou dynasty, attained a far-reaching distribution, examples of it occurring at Teotihuacán itself, in the highlands and on the Pacific slope of Guatemala, and as far as the Ulua Valley of eastern Honduras. Part of this spread may postdate the fall of Teotihuacán, since El Tajín appears to survive the highland metropolis by several centuries. It may also be speculated that El Tajín was a major competitor to Teotihuacán in the cacao trade and a principal beneficiary of the latter's collapse.

Like Teotihuacán, Monte Albán in the Southern Highlands may have been a true city, and perhaps a very large one. It continues in Classic times to be the seat of the distinctive tradition that was seen emerging in the earlier phases I and II. Its individuality is manifest in the elaboration of tomb construction, the development of distinctive architectural conventions, the carving of stelae with inscriptions, representations of local deities, the style of its large effigy vessels generally referred to as "urns" (at first sober, later extremely ornate), and local pottery forms. In phase III-A, local traits mingle with many of Teotihuacán origin, most particularly in pottery and in the style of small greenstone figurines. In III-B, Teotihuacán features disappear, probably at the same time as they do elsewhere in Mesoamerica (c. A.D. 550), and relative cultural isolation sets in, though some contact with the Lowland Mayas is evident. Unlike the Teotihuacán and the Tajín traditions, that of Monte Albán appears to have had limited impact outside of its home range in Oaxaca. And unlike those traditions, whose authorship is conjectural (though it is often speculated that Nahua and Totonac speakers may have participated in both), Monte Albán can, with reasonable assurance, be attributed to a known ethnic group, the Zapotecs, who inhabited eastern Oaxaca at the time of the Spanish Conquest.

Beyond the Isthmus, we enter the Maya area. Highland and Pacific Guatemala onward seem dominated, to an unusual degree, by cultures emanating from Mexico, and the promise implicit in the Miraflores phase, that of cultural development closely parallel to that of the Maya lowlands, remains unrealized. This seems particularly true of the Early Classic, when architecture and pottery strongly suggest the presence of overlords from Teotihuacán, but it holds also for Late Classic, when evidence is pervasive of links with Veracruz. By contrast, the lowlands of the Petén, neighboring Chiapas and Tabasco and, farther north, the Yucatán Peninsula

Based on an illustration in Miguel Covarrubias, *Indian Art of Mexico and Central America* (New York: Knopf, 1957). Copyright © 1957 by Alfred A. Knopf, Inc. Used by permission of the publisher.

FIGURE 2.5   Relief with inscriptions from the site of Palenque, Chiapas, Lowland Maya region, Late Classic period (A.D. 600–900).

see the florescence of the very distinctive Lowland Maya tradition (Figure 2.5). It takes form during the Chicanel phase of the Late Preclassic and is represented in Classic times by hundreds of sites, many of them with stone buildings, monuments and inscriptions.

Though some sites, like Tikal, extend over many square kilometers, none appears to have been a crowded city. Like other lowland sites, these were evidently ceremonial, and probably administrative, centers for broad "sustaining areas." Size and distribution patterns of sites suggest the existence of minor "zones," served by smaller centers, and larger "districts," in which several zones were grouped around a major center. Inscriptions similarly hint that smaller ceremonial centers may have been politically dependent on the larger ones. The two most common types of building are temples, typically on tall, steep pyramids, and multiroomed "palaces," on somewhat lower platforms. Both kinds are usually integrated into an overall plan of terraces, courts, and stairways. Set into the courts and terraces are stone monuments (stelae and altars), often carved and inscribed with hieroglyphic texts and dates. Those portions of the texts that are understood reveal, not only a calendar more elaborate than that used in most other parts of Mesoamerica, but also the performance of complex calculations and a body of accurate astronomical knowledge. Portions still undeciphered may deal with dynastic history, and their abundance promises considerable contributions to our understanding of the Mayas once they can be read.

Though perhaps the most distinctive of the four major traditions of the Classic, that of the Lowland Mayas, did not remain isolated from trends in other parts of Mesoamerica. Early Classic pottery at Tikal not only contains imports and copies of Teotihuacán vessels, but reliefs at that site include a representation of Tlaloc and that of an armed individual, both of them clearly from the Central Highlands of Mexico. In the Late Classic, perhaps upon the decline of Teotihuacán, Maya influence extends outward to southern Veracruz (affecting particularly the "smiling face" style of Las Remojadas) and to highland Oaxaca.

South and east of the Lowland Maya border in western Honduras, Maya culture appears to have been influential, as evident from polychrome pottery styles that extend as far south as Costa Rica. It is difficult to decide whether this southern frontier region is to be included in Mesoamerica at this time. The answer may become clearer when we have a concrete understanding of the nature of the links that bound it to the Maya and other societies to the north.

The other frontier region of Mesoamerica, the one in the desert north, appears to have been expanding in Classic times. Sites such as La Quemada and Chalchihuites in Zacatecas during the Alta Vista phase (A.D. 350–550) and the somewhat later site of Zape in Durango show Mesoamerican civilization moving north along the eastern slopes of the western Sierra Madre. They may represent colonists using local labor to mine materials needed by the lapidaries of Mesoamerica. Contact with local subsistence farmers and with nomads of the Northern Plateau probably brought about the transmission of many Mesoamerican traits into the North American Southwest at this time. The weakening and eventual collapse of this northern frontier, on the other hand, was to affect profoundly the core of Mesoamerica in later times.

In sum, the Classic is the period in which Mesoamerica, as a whole, appears to have raised its overall level of economic development and societal complexity to the mark set by the Olmecs in Veracruz some 1,200 years earlier. It is also the time of appearance of a new kind of organism, typified by Teotihuacán, which in size, in power, and in administrative complexity transcends this generally shared level. Teotihuacán was an irrigation-based, urban, conquest-state, which directly controlled regions as remote as highland Guatemala and as environmentally alien as the southern Gulf coast. Though its domination ceases or becomes severely curtailed in Late Classic times, it probably provided the direct model for the states that were to compete for power in the succeeding Postclassic, just as the Olmec had originally provided the pattern for the Classic societies.

· CONFLICTS AND CONQUESTS OF THE
POSTCLASSIC (A.D. 900–1520)

Native chronicles, many of them written shortly after the Conquest, narrate events, and contain dates and the names of ethnic groups, persons, and places prominent in the political history of Mesoamerica in the eight centuries or so preceding Spanish arrival. In the light of these documents, it is easy to exaggerate the unstable and episodic quality of the Postclassic, seemingly replete with warfare and population movements. Yet, and despite inadequate spadework on the part of archaeologists, there is some independent evidence to support these accounts and to suggest that the Postclassic was indeed a time of ascendant militarism and political up-heaval. The Central Highlands continue in their key role, acquired in the Classic, with the difference that now the region seems in-creasingly affected by developments on its own northern frontier.

A major tradition, commonly designated as Mixteca-Puebla, emerges in central Mexico after the fall of Teotihuacán. It domi-nates, in the form of a series of related subtraditions, not only the Central Highlands, but also adjacent portions of the Gulf coast, of the Southern Highlands, and of western and northwestern Mex-ico. It is identified by a repertory of motifs and symbols, many of them of long standing in Mesoamerica but now found in new combinations or given new emphasis. Warfare, human sacrifice, death tend to be emphasized, as is the worship of deities whose precise identity and insignia are known to us from surviving native picture books or codices and post-Conquest commentaries upon them. The tradition is most famed as a style of painting on pottery, plaster, and paper but can be recognized in sculpture, architecture, ritual, and other cultural expressions. In the Central Highlands, its major center was at first Cholula, on the broad plain of Puebla, a city already in existence in the Classic. Its pyramid, twice en-larged, became in Postclassic times greater in bulk than the Pyra-mid of the Sun of Teotihuacán. According to some of the sources, Cholula was the capital of the Olmeca-Xicalanca, a lineage from the Gulf coast whose political domination over part of the Central Highlands lasted five centuries.

On the Gulf coast, Mixteca-Puebla themes are evident in the reliefs at El Tajín and in the pottery of Isla de Sacrificios, and there is even some possibility that such traits go back further in time in Veracruz than elsewhere. To the north, the Huasteca now gives clear evidence of having joined Mesoamerica, the Las Flores (Panuco V) phase there being marked by major sites, stone sculp-ture, and stylistic links with the Mixteca-Puebla tradition.

To the south, the hilltop center of Xochicalco overlooking the plain of Morelos may actually be Late Classic and predate the emergence of the Mixteca-Puebla tradition. Its defensive features (walls and moats) suggest already unsettled political conditions. The glyphs and carvings, highly eclectic in style, indicate contact with all major traditions of the terminal Classic, including the

Maya. Farther south and east, the Mixtec states, whose known dynastic history goes back to A.D. 692, come to participate in the Mixteca-Puebla tradition and begin to expand through western Oaxaca and eventually into the valley of Oaxaca itself.

Culturally, the entities so far mentioned (with the exception of Xochicalco, which stands apart) may be viewed together and contrasted with another, somewhat deviant manifestation of the Mixteca-Puebla tradition, found at Tula and at numerous sites in western and northwestern Mexico, a region whose integration into Mesoamerica, probably begun in Classic times, now becomes complete. Tula, itself, on an arid plain some 60 kilometers north of the Basin of Mexico, is known to have been the capital of the politically powerful Toltecs. The architecture, sculpture, and certain other traits at Tula suggest the fusion of a Teotihuacán heritage with Mixteca Puebla elements. The pottery, however, is basically quite different and in a tradition ultimately going back to Chupícuaro and, beyond it, perhaps to Tlatilco. Similar pottery, in which red-on-brown decoration and the tall tripod bowl are important features, is known from Classic sites in Guanajuato (Morales phase) and in Zacatecas. Postclassic sites with related red-on-buff ceramics, Tula-like figurines, and such specialized items (also found at Tula) as chili graters, handled censers, and pipes occur far to the west in the Lerma-Santiago basin (Cojumatlán, Amapá), in Colima, and as far north as Sinaloa (Chametla, Culiacán). This is also the time when metal-working appears in Mesoamerica, and parts of western Mexico become major centers of that craft.

Though probably in competition with the Olmeca-Xicalancas based in Cholula, the Toltecs were the major power in the Central Highlands in the early Postclassic. According to one source, they controlled the Basin of Mexico even before the founding of Tula, which must have taken place A.D. 950 at the latest but may well have taken place earlier. In A.D. 1045, the authority of Tula is acknowledged by the Mixtec sovereign, Eight Deer. Farther south and east, however, Toltec power does not seem to have reached directly. Nevertheless, the events and trends of the Central Highlands affected profoundly both highland Guatemala and the Lowland Maya region from *c.* A.D. 900 onward.

Thus, in some parts of the Guatemala highlands, valley settlements and ceremonial centers are abandoned in favor of defensively located hilltop sites, whereas others become depopulated altogether, as is most of the Pacific slope. Native accounts speak of warlike intruders from Mexico, and Mixteca-Puebla influence is manifest in architecture and pottery alike. In the Petén lowlands, the Maya ceremonial centers cease to be maintained by the end of the ninth century. The Petén becomes, if not deserted, at least thoroughly rural. Whether this should be attributed to Mexican marauders is uncertain, though, in view of events to the south and north, military incursions by outsiders are likely to have occurred. To the north, on the Yucatán Peninsula, a dense population and building activity are indicated, but, as in Guatemala, Mexican features are visible from A.D. 900 onward, particularly in architecture, and there are traditional accounts of the arrival of Toltec war parties. Central Highland sources suggest, in this particular case, that the intruders may have been a splinter group that left Tula in the tenth century under a leader named One Reed, whose title was Feathered Serpent. At the site of Chichén Itzá, a number of buildings, probably erected at this time, show such precise correspondences with Tula that they can be seen as conscious attempts to reproduce portions of that site.

The full impact of the Toltecs among both the Highland and Lowland Mayas may be gauged from the fact that, at Conquest times, some ruling lineages in both regions still claimed Toltec descent. Neither region, however, achieved political stability in Postclassic times, and small warring states existed at Spanish arrival, perpetuating an impoverished version of the Classic Maya tradition with a Mexican overlay going back to Toltec times.

In the meantime, Tula is sacked, probably in the twelfth century, by raiders from the north. They, and the other groups called "Chichimecs," mentioned in the sources as barbarian nomads, may have been, in the main, dispossessed marginal farmers from the northern frontier zone, perhaps displaced by drought. The fall of Tula and the Chichimec intrusions that followed appear to coincide in time with the abandonment of the frontier sites in Durango and Zacatecas founded in Classic times.

The fall of Tula initiates a century or more of dislocation, in which groups of refugees from formerly Toltec territory or from farther north spill onto the central plateau and beyond, some founding new communities, others settling in existing ones and often gaining control of them as new ruling lineages.

In western Mexico, these events may be linked with the introduction of new Mixteca-Puebla features on the Pacific coastal plain as far north as Guasave, in Sinaloa, and with the founding of the Tarascan kingdom in Michoacán. To the south, in Guatemala, some of the self-styled Toltec lineages may appear now rather than earlier. In the Central Highlands, Cholula falls, and, in the south, the Mixtecs occupy the valley of Oaxaca.

The Basin of Mexico receives a succession of invaders identified in the accounts as Chichimecs, Acolhuas, and Tenochcas, the last-named, also known as the Mexicas or Aztecs, founding a community on an island in Lake Texcoco *c.* A.D. 1325. This community grew on ground reclaimed from the lake until, in 1500, its population equaled or exceeded that of the earlier Teotihuacán. This, of course, was Tenochtitlán, today, Mexico City.

Aztec culture, as we know it archaeologically, with its characteristic black-on-orange pottery, its massive and often forbidding stone sculpture (Figure 2.6), and its religion notable for its devotion to human sacrifice, is a variant of the Mixteca-Puebla tradition. It apparently emerged in Toltec times in such communities as Culhuacán and Chalco, in the south of the Basin of Mexico. The Tenochcas came to share this subtradition with a number of other lakeside towns, inserting themselves into a pre-existing, relatively prosperous society that sustained itself through a variety of farming techniques (*chinampas,* canal irrigation, hillside cultivation with humidity-conservation techniques). In 1430, the Aztecs formed the politically powerful Triple Alliance with the communities of Texcoco and Tacuba and came to control that alliance by 1500. The alliance waged a series of military campaigns, first within the highlands, then as far as both coasts and across the Isthmus of Tehuantepec into the cacao-producing coastal plains of Chiapas and Guatemala. When Cortés landed in 1519, much of Mesoamerica, though not the Maya regions, had become a vast though loose empire, with many local societies in a tributary relationship to the Aztec state.

It is important to emphasize, however, not only that several

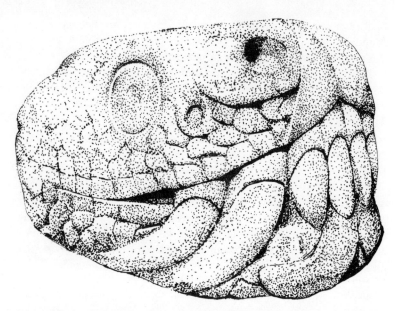

FIGURE 2.6   Representation of snake head in the round. A typical
example of Aztec sculpture (15th or early 16th century).

important states, such as Tlaxcala and the Tarascan kingdom, were
resisting the Aztecs militarily in 1519, but that many of the other
subject peoples were under very imperfect control. Punitive expe-
ditions were frequently needed to ensure the payment of tribute
and the maintenance of trade routes. The looseness and brevity of
Aztec dominion over Mesoamerica, interrupted in 1520, are re-
flected in the thinness of the archaeological evidence, particularly
outside of the Central Highlands. In this light, one is led back to
reflect on the nature of the Teotihuacán empire. In A.D. 500 it may
have been a structure considerably sounder than any known in
Mesoamerica from historical or eyewitness accounts. In contrast
to the Aztecs, the Teotihuacán empire seems to have been well
integrated, long-lived, and free from incessant warfare. The Teoti-
huacanos built and managed their domain with efficiency and
appear not to have been harassed by the constant threats to their
control that marked Aztec administration.

· BIBLIOGRAPHIC ESSAY

The original definition of Mesoamerica was given by Paul Kirchhoff in 1943 and has been reprinted more recently in John A. Graham, ed., *Ancient Mesoamerica, Selected Readings* (Palo Alto, Calif.: Peek Publications, 1966). This collection also includes 29 other articles, dealing with many aspects of the prehistory of Mesoamerica. A general appraisal of environments, major food resources, and their possible roles in the rise of Mesoamerican civilization is to be found in *Mesoamerica: The Evolution of a Civilization,* by William T. Sanders and Barbara J. Price, Random House Studies in Anthropology, AS 9 (New York, 1968). See also the review by Paul Tolstoy in *American Anthropologist,* Vol. 71, No. 3 (1969), pp. 554–58.

Environmental and preceramic data for the Tehuacán Valley are presented in the first two volumes of Douglas S. Byers, ed., *The Prehistory of the Tehuacán Valley* (Austin and London: University of Texas Press, 1967, 1968); see particularly the summary sections by Richard S. MacNeish. The emergence of farming as the mainstay of subsistence in the highlands is examined by Kent V. Flannery in "Archeological Systems Theory and Early Mesoamerica," a paper that appears in the volume *Anthropological Archeology in the Americas,* published by the Anthropological Society of Washington (Washington, D.C., 1968), pp. 67–87. For the lowlands, somewhat different conditions for the beginnings of village life are suggested by Mac-Neish ("Mesoamerican Archaeology," in *Biennial Review of Anthropology,* 1967, edited by Bernard J. Siegel and Alan R. Beals, Stanford University Press, pp. 326–28) and, less directly, by Michael D. Coe and Kent V. Flannery in "Microenvironments and Mesoamerican Prehistory" (reprinted in Graham's *Selected Readings,* cited above, pp. 46–50).

Purrón pottery is described by R. S. MacNeish *et al.* in *Ceramics,* Vol. 3 of *The Prehistory of the Tehuacán Valley* (Austin: University of Texas Press, 1970), pp. 21–25. Pox pottery is the subject of a brief note by Charles F. Brush in *Science,* Vol. 149, No. 3680 (1965), pp. 194–95. Early phases of the Isthmian region are discussed by Gareth W. Lowe in Dee F. Green and Gareth W. Lowe, *Altamira and Padre Piedra, Early Preclassic Sites in Chiapas, Mexico,* Papers of the New World Archaeological Foundation, No. 20 (Provo, Utah, 1967), pp. 53–79.

An overview of the Olmec problem is given in an attractive book by Michael D. Coe, *America's First Civilization,* published by American Heritage Publishing Co. and The Smithsonian Institution in 1968. Further discussion of Olmec remains in various parts of Mesoamerica is to be found in Elizabeth P. Benson, ed., *Dumbarton Oaks Conference on the Olmec* (Washington, D.C.: Dumbarton Oaks Research Library and Collection, 1968) and, for the Basin of Mexico, in an article by Paul Tolstoy and Louise Paradis, "Early and Middle Preclassic Culture in the Basin of Mexico," *Science,* Vol. 167, No. 3917 (1970), pp. 344–51.

The literature on Mesoamerica after the Olmecs is immense. Eric Wolf's *Sons of the Shaking Earth,* Phoenix Books, P90 (Chicago: University of Chicago Press, 1962), remains one of the best syntheses, despite being somewhat out of date. Other good general books include Miguel Covarrubias, *Indian Art of Mexico and Central America* (New York: Knopf, 1957); Michael D. Coe, *Mexico* (New York: Praeger, 1962); *The Maya,* by the same author (New York: Praeger, 1966); the collection of readings edited by John Graham cited earlier; and, for the Maya, J. Eric S. Thompson's *The Rise and Fall of Maya Civilization* (Norman: University of Oklahoma Press, 1966). More detailed coverage of archaeological materials is to be found in Volumes 2, 3, and 4 of Robert Wauchope, ed., *Handbook of Middle American Indians* (Austin: University of Texas Press, 1965–66) and is forthcoming in volumes that are to follow Vol. 9. Unfortunately, some of this material is already out of date. Recent work at Teotihuacán has been summarized in the volume *Teotihuacán* (Onceava Mesa Redonda, Mexico: Sociedad Mexicana de Antropología, 1966), and in an article by René Millon in *Science,* Vol. 170, No. 3962 (1970), pp. 1077–82. The history of the Toltecs and Aztecs is sketched by Ignacio Bernal in his *Mexico Before Cortez,* Dolphin Books (New York: Doubleday, 1963), Chs. 6–8. The systematic but naive description of Aztec society by George C. Vaillant in *Aztecs of Mexico,* Pelican Books, A200 (Harmondsworth, Middlesex, 1950) should be supplemented through a reading of Robert McC. Adams' *The Evolution of Urban Society* (Chicago: Aldine, 1966), which attempts a comparison between early Mesopotamian and Mesoamerican civilizations, and of the relevant sections of the works of Wolf and of Sanders and Price cited earlier.

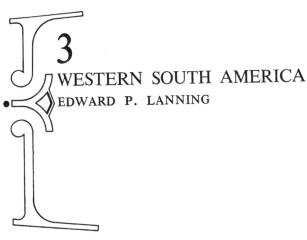

3
WESTERN SOUTH AMERICA
EDWARD P. LANNING

The western side of South America is dominated by the Andes, the great chain of mountains that extends from northwestern Venezuela nearly to the southern tip of the continent. Formidable as these mighty mountains appear when one flies over them, they are not inhospitable to man. Rivers have created large, fertile valleys with excellent soils for farming. High plateaus provide abundant pastureland for both wild and domestic animals. The forested eastern slopes (the *montaña*) allow the cultivation of hot-climate plants almost within walking distance of highlands settlements.

The coastal plain to the west of the Andes offers a variety of environments. The Pacific coast of Colombia is a hot, wet, tropical forest where rainfall may reach 400 inches per year. After a rapid transition along the Ecuadorian coast, one enters one of the world's driest deserts, extending along the entire coast of Peru and the northern half of the Chilean coast. In Peru this desert is crossed by many small rivers that head in the mountains and that have extremely fertile valleys; in Chile it is practically barren and extends far up into the highlands. The coastal plain disappears in southern Chile, where pine-clad mountains slope directly down to the sea and are fringed by hundreds of rocky islands.

Most of the archaeological research in the Andean area has been carried on in its central portion—southern Ecuador, Peru, western Bolivia, northern Chile, and northwestern Argentina. Investigations in this relatively well-studied sector, however, have been rather unbalanced. In general, we know most about the desert

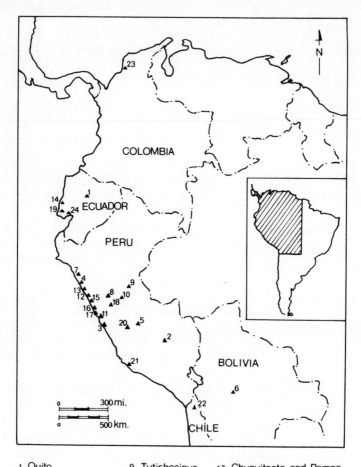

1. Quito	9. Tutishcainyo	17. Chuquitanta and Pampa
2. Cuzco	10. Kotosh	18. Lauricocha
3. Pachacamac	11. La Florida	19. Las Vegas
4. Chan Chan	12. Las Haldas	20. Ayacucho
5. Huari	13. Cerro Sechín	21. Ica Nazca
6. Tiahuanaco	14. Valdívia	22. Quiani
7. Moche	15. Culebras	23. Puerto Hormiga
8. Chavín de Huantar	16. Río Seco	24. La Libertad

MAP 3.1   Archaeological sites in western South America.

coast, considerably less about most of the highlands, and very little indeed about the eastern slopes of the Andes. The people of each of these broad environmental zones made important contributions to the ancient Andean cultures, but the unevenness of the research inevitably leads one to stress those zones for which we have the most information (Map 3.1).

The Pleistocene cultures of the Andes are still difficult to date with any precision. For the post-Pleistocene, though, we have many well-known archaeological sequences dated by stratigraphy and radiocarbon. Chart 3.1 gives a selection of nine of the best-defined regional sequences, broken down into standard pan-Andean periods.

During the early post-Pleistocene the entire area, with the possible exception of the *montaña,* was inhabited by small bands of nomadic hunters and food gatherers. Though these bands presumably had established territories and fixed seasonal rounds, we cannot yet trace their movements in more than a general way. On the central coast of Peru, for example, from Arenal through Encanto times, they spent their winters in the *lomas*—meadows fed by the winter fogs—gathering roots and seeds, hunting occasional deer, and doing some fishing and shellfishing along the shore. At least some of these *lomas* dwellers spent at least part of their summers in the coastal river valleys, but they may also have migrated up into the nearby highlands when the *lomas* dried out for the year.

Some of the Peruvian highlands dwellers moved up to extremely high altitudes to hunt guanaco during the summers. The Lauricocha caves, for example, lie near 15,000 feet of altitude. They contain ancient refuse packed with guanaco bones and hunting gear. Winters were spent at lower altitudes, around or below 10,000 feet, where the meat diet was probably supplemented by substantial gathering of plant foods.

The Vegas people of coastal Ecuador spent the summer wet season gathering food along inland creeks and the winter dry season living by coastal lagoons, where they gathered shellfish and hunted such animals as peccaries. In the northern Chilean highlands, from Isla Grande through Chiu Chiu times, the main sources of meat were camelids, mainly guanaco but possibly also the domestic llama. Field mice and rhizomes were also important parts of the

	ECUADOR	PERU	COAST	
	SOUTH COAST	NORTH COAST	CENTRAL COAST	SOUTH COAST
1500	Libertad	Inca	Inca	Tararacu
		Chimú	Chancay	Soniche
1000		Santa		Chulpaca
		Patiuilca	Pachacamac	Epigonal Atarca
500	Guangala		Lima	Nazca
1		Patazca	Miramar	
			Ventanilla	
500	Engoroy	Pallka	San Bartob	Paracas
1000	Machalilla	Gualaño	Colinas	Mastodonte
		Cahuacucho		
	Valdívia	Haldas	Chira	Hacha
2000		Culebras	Gaviota	Casavilea
			Conchas	
			Playa Hermosa	
			Pampa	
3000			Encanto	
4000			Corvina	
			Canario	
5000			Arenal-Luz	
6000	Vegas			
7000				
8000				

CHART 3.1   Phases of western South American culture.

HIGHLANDS				BOLIVIA
CALLEJON DE HUAYLAS	**KOTOSH**	**YARINACOCHA**	**AYACUCHO**	**TIAHUANACO**
Huaman Huilca	Marabamba	Caimito	Qotu Qotu	Palli Marca
Aquilpo	Marabamba	Caimito		Wancani
Honco		Cumancaya		
Huaylas	Higueras	Nueva Esperanza / Cashibocaño	Viñaque / Chaquipampa	Tiahuanaco
Huaylas	Higueras	Pacacocha	Huarpa	Qeya
Huaylas	Higueras	Yarinacocha	Aya Orjo	Qeya
Huaylas	Kotosh White on Red	Hupa-Iya	Rancha	Qalasasaya
Chavín / Copilla	San Blas	Late Shakimu	Rancha	Late Chiripa
Chavín / Copilla	Sajarapatac	Late Shakimu		Late Chiripa
Chavín / Copilla	Kotosh Chavín	Early Shakimu	Wichgana	Late Chiripa
Toril	Kotosh	Late Tutishcainyo		Early Chiripa
Toril	Huairajirca	Late Tutishcainyo		Early Chiripa
Lauricocha III		Early Tutishcainyo		Viscachani
Lauricocha II	Ambo			Viscachani
Lauricocha I				

diet. Nomadism in this area was not controlled by seasonal ripening of different food resources because the major food sources were available all year round. Rather, in this driest of all deserts, food of any sort could be had only in narrow strips of pastureland along either side of the few rivers, and a small band of people had to move continuously along 40 to 50 miles of river land to keep from exhausting the food supply in any one place.

During Periods III–V (*c.* 8000–2600 B.C.), tools and weapons were made of stone, bone, wood, and shell, but only those of stone have been preserved in any great quantity. These include, in Peru and Chile, projectile points, knives, skin scrapers, rough scrapers and scraper planes for working wood and fiber, perforators, awls, choppers, mortars, pestles, milling stones, and *manos*. The Vegas complex of Ecuador represents a different, northern tradition. Its stone tools are almost entirely for wood working: little denticulates, spokeshaves, gravers, and rough scrapers. In this well-watered coastal region, more distinctive artifacts were probably all made of bamboo and mangrove wood, which have not been preserved in the archaeological sites.

The first hints of change in this basic lifeway are found about 5000 B.C., halfway through Period IV. At this time cultivated plants first appear in the archaeological records of the south highlands and central coast of Peru. They include gourds in the coastal Canario complex and gourds, quinoa (a native grain), and possibly squash in the highlands Piki complex. Domestic llamas and guinea pigs have also been reported from the Piki complex. The llama may have been still older in the northern Chilean highlands, but this is by no means certain.

Cultivation was practiced in Mexico at an earlier date than its first known appearance in Peru, but the earliest shared cultigens—gourds and squash—appeared at about the same time in both areas. They could have been brought under cultivation independently; they could have been first cultivated in an intermediate area and spread both ways; or the idea and techniques could have spread southward from Mexico and have been applied to native species in Peru. I do not favor a hypothesis of totally independent invention of farming in the two areas, but there is at present no way of arriving at a firm conclusion. So far we do not have any preserved plant remains of comparable antiquity anywhere between southern Mexico and central Peru. Until they are found, the history of American agriculture will be a barely opened book.

The adoption of cultigens and domesticate animals seems to have had no great impact on life in either the highlands or the lowlands for several millennia. For some time it led neither to significant population growth nor to sedentary lifeways; rather, crop plants (and apparently also llamas and guinea pigs) were but a minor supplement to the roster of wild plants and animals on which the Andean Indians depended.

To be sure, the earliest permanent sedentary villages were built about 4200 B.C., at the beginning of Period V, but they were on the coast of northern Chile, where food production was not yet known. The one firmly dated village site of this time is a shell-mound at Quiani, just to the south of the last Peru-type coastal river valley and to the north of the endless wastes of the northern Chilean desert. Its inhabitants lived mainly by fishing and shell-fishing. Shell fishhooks and stone sinkers are common in the early levels of Quiani, but projectile points and a few mats of reeds and rushes suggest that the inhabitants occasionally trekked northward to the river to hunt and gather useful plants.

Even while Peruvian lifeways were undergoing no basic changes, new plants were occasionally brought under cultivation. Lúcuma (a native fruit), squash, maize, and cotton are found in the Chihua complex of the southern highlands, while maize, beans, and jack beans first appear in the Cachi complex about 2700 B.C. Jack beans, several varieties of squash, and guava appeared in the Pampa complex of the central coast, to be followed immediately by cotton and chili peppers in Playa Hermosa. By 1700 or 1800 B.C. all of these plants except quinoa were being grown in one place or another on the coast, as were lima beans and sweet potatoes, while coca was probably being imported from the *montaña*.

About 2500 B.C. the coastal peoples began abandoning their nomadic lifeway and settling in permanent sedentary villages along the shore. The earliest village yet known in Peru is the Pampa site, but others were built all along the Peruvian coast during the ensuing centuries. The population began to grow rapidly until, by shortly after 2000 B.C., there was a little village on almost every good fishing beach or rocky point. Many of these settlements were located at or near the mouths of river valleys, but others were situated out on the desert coast far from fresh water and potential farm land.

Regardless of site location, subsistence at this time came primarily from the shore. Refuse heaps are packed with mollusc shells, bones of fish, shore birds, and sea lions, and crab and tunicate remains. Cotton and gourds are abundant, usually in the form of twined and looped cotton cloth and of gourd containers and net floats. Plant foods—either wild or cultivated—seldom make up much of the middens. One pictures a people harvesting the shore on a year-round basis and growing only enough food on the delta lands to supplement their high-protein diet, with the barest minimum of trade in crop foods to the more remote desert settlements (Figure 3.1).

About 1900 B.C. this situation began to change. As the better habitats along the shore were occupied, excess population began to move inland into the valleys, establishing full-time farming villages that traded much of their produce to the shore dwellers for fish and shellfish. At the same time, many of the coastal dwellers began to build in stone and adobe, and some of their constructions represented community effort on a considerable scale. At the Culebras site, on the north-central coast and contemporary with the Gaviota complex, a large hillside was leveled off into numerous stone-faced terraces, on each of which were built three or four stone-walled semi-subterranean houses. At the Gaviota site of Chuquitanta in the Chillón Valley, two "apartment houses" up to 450 yards long were built to flank a great patio. A smaller structure at the head of the patio may have been a temple. Either of these sites could have housed up to 1,000 people—substantial towns indeed when compared to the little villages that preceded them.

Still more striking is the Gaviota site of Río Seco, in the desert to the north of the Chancay Valley. Houses here were made of adobe and probably also of such perishable material as wattle-and-daub. But two pyramids, made of adobe and boulders, are the oldest known example in the Americas of public architecture on any considerable scale. These pyramids may have been a focus of

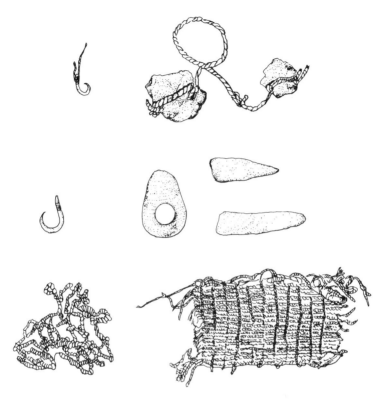

FIGURE 3.1   Pampa and farmer-fisher village artifacts.

worship for the people of a fairly large region. For hundreds of yards around them, the ground is full of offering pits containing foodstuffs, tools, cotton cloth, mats, and incised sticks and bones.

Meanwhile, cultural evolution in the northern Andes was taking quite a different course. We know virtually nothing about the Ecuadorian and Colombian highlands on this time level, but we have a fair picture of life along the coast. The population was scattered out in small villages along the edges of lagoons, exploiting the mangrove environment as had their ancestors, but apparently (at least in the case of the Valdívia people) also cultivating some crops, including maize. There is no sign of the increasing population

density, exploitation of new environments, permanent constructions, or public buildings that characterized Peru at this time. On
the other hand, they were making and using pottery and, in Ecuador, figurines. Pottery-making first appeared at Puerto Hormiga on
the Caribbean coast of Colombia about 3100 B.C. By 2800 B.C.
it had spread to the Ecuadorian coast, where the Valdívia complex is noted for its elaborate incised, excised, appliqué, and
textured wares. Figurines made of stone appeared in Valdívia
about 2400 B.C., and clay female figurines followed soon after.

The antiquity and origins of this early pottery-making and of
the figurine cult are not now known. It has been proposed that
both were brought from Japan by a fishing boat that had been
blown off course, but the bulk of our present evidence rather suggests a point of origin for the pottery somewhere in the interior
of the northern Andes or perhaps out in the lowland tropical forest.
If so, we can expect to find much older pottery in the area than
that now known. The figurines, on the other hand, could well have
been invented on the Ecuadorian coast, where a series of antecedent stone forms has been shown to exist.

Pottery-making spread slowly into Peru, probably by several
routes through the highlands and the *montaña*. It filtered down to
the central coast about 1750 B.C., to the north and south coasts
about 1500 B.C., and into the Bolivian highlands by 1300 B.C.
During the same period the heddle loom—probably invented about
1800 B.C.—was spreading across Peru, and woven cloth quickly
replaced the older twined and looped kinds. There is some reason
to believe that the two crafts, weaving and pottery-making, spread
together through much of the central Andes.

The Initial Period in Peru (*c.* 1750–900 B.C.) was a time of
intensification and spreading out of the processes that had got
underway in late preceramic times. Maize, llamas, and guinea pigs
now spread throughout most of ancient Peru. The coastal populations continued to grow and to fill up the valleys, which gradually
grew more important as demographic and cultural centers. Pyramids and temples were built here and there along the central and
north-central coast, from Lima to the Casma Valley, and in the
north-central highlands eastward nearly to the *montaña*. Village
life spread southward into Bolivia. It is likely that population

growth in the highlands began to accelerate at this time, though there is no clear evidence on the subject.

Of eight Initial Period ceremonial sites known in central and north-central Peru, four are particularly interesting. At La Florida, in the modern city of Lima, a great pyramid about 110 feet high and nearly 1,000 feet long was begun about 1750 B.C. and probably completed by about 1700 B.C. At Las Haldas, on the desert coast to the south of the Casma Valley, a large temple complex was begun (and probably completed) shortly before 1600 B.C. The temple buildings, of modest size, occupied a small terraced hillside. Three great stone-walled plazas stretch out before them. The whole complex measures about 700 by 200 yards and is approached by an entrance highway running more than a mile through the desert. Two smaller temples are noteworthy for the first appearance of architectural decoration. At Cerro Sechín in the Casma Valley (only tentatively dated to the Initial Period) there are numerous incised stone stelae apparently showing the victors and vanquished in a local war. At Kotosh in the eastern highlands, a temple wall built before 1450 B.C. is ornamented with a bas relief of crossed human hands.

None of these sites had much of a population in residence. Especially at the great centers of La Florida and Las Haldas, it is evident that the labor of several communities went into the construction and probably also the subsequent upkeep. It would seem that even at this early date we are dealing with the centralized authority patterns that we are fond of calling "states" or "civilizations." In terms to be used later in this book, these were small-scale Rural Nucleated states, in which a dispersed rural society was ruled from "empty" ceremonial centers, while commerce and manufacture were carried on primarily in the countryside. In the case of La Florida, the state need not have encompassed more than the deltas of the Chillón and Rimac rivers; in the case of Las Haldas, those of the Casma and Culebras rivers.

During the Initial Period, then, there was a nuclear area of stratified societies and incipient states in central and north-central Peru. In southern Peru and the Bolivian highlands, and in the northern Andes, little farming and/or fishing villages were proliferating, but there is no evidence of a change toward intercommunity authority patterns. In the interior of northern Chile, people still carried on the old nomadic lifeway, hunting and gathering wild foods. The archaeological record of the *montaña,* insofar as it is known at all, begins in the Initial Period with pottery-making villages. Their influence in the centers of incipient civilization is seen in the popularity of such tropical plants as coca, manioc, and peanuts. Interestingly, the earliest of these villages, Tutishcainyo, seems to have been in close contact with Kotosh, the easternmost early ceremonial center.

About 900 B.C. a religious cult and its art style spread out of the nuclear area across much of ancient Peru. This cult is known as Chavín, after its most famous temple at Chavín de Huantar in the north-central highlands. The period from the first spread of the Chavín cult to the disappearance of the last vestiges of its influence lasted from about 900 to 250 B.C. and is known as the Early Horizon.

The Chavín art style is found in stone carvings, pottery, textiles, gold, and carved shell and bone (Figure 3.2). Humans, jaguars, eagles, and hawks were the principal subjects represented, but alligators, crabs, snakes, fish, and bats are not unknown. Some of the most famous pieces represent one or the other of two deities, the Staff God and the Smiling God, which combine human and feline characteristics. There is no doubt of the religious nature of much of this art. The finest examples of it are the friezes, lintels, columns, stelae, altars, and cult objects of the major Chavín temples.

Art objects, especially pottery, in Chavín style are found in archaeological sites throughout the coast and highlands of central and northern Peru. Temples, all apparently built to the same ground plan and most ornamented in Chavín style, are scattered throughout the same area. Probably all of these structures, and all of the specimens in pure Chavín style, date between 900 and 500 B.C. On the south coast, where Chavín temples and the pure Chavín style did not penetrate, the Paracas potters and weavers took over the human and animal figures and made them the central themes of their art. Within the boundaries of modern Peru, only the *montaña* and the southern highlands seem to have lain outside the area of Chavín influence.

The spread of the Chavín style was undoubtedly associated with

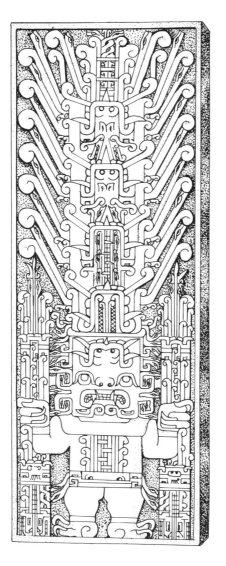

Based on an illustration in Julio Tello, *Chavín: Cultura Matriz de la Civilización Andina* (Lima, Peru: Universidad de San Marcos, 1960).

FIGURE 3.2   Chavín stone carving.

the expansion of a religious cult, but the full nature of the phenomenon remains a mystery. Was the religion spread by the sword?
Was the cult widely worshiped before the art style evolved? Could
a few missionaries have so quickly made converts of more than
half the people of Peru? We have no answers to these questions,
but the distribution of art objects does suggest something about
the nature of society within Chavín territory. Though the famous
masterpieces come mostly from temples, everyday objects like pots
and textiles in purest Chavín style can be found in even the meanest
village occupied between 900 and about 500 B.C. These specimens
probably represent trade in luxury goods for the upper classes, and
their distribution suggests a society whose leaders formed an interacting network penetrating to and resident in every settlement in
Chavín territory. In such a society, there need have been no capital
or any central government above the regional level. The village
higher-ups and the priests in the temples would have governed
together and may even have been blood relatives.

Insofar as the Chavín expansion had an impact on aspects of life
other than religion and art, it was in extending the nuclear area of
Peruvian civilization. It was at this time that the Rural Nucleated
type of state organization spread northward almost to the boundary
of modern Peru and southward somewhat beyond its Initial Period
limits.

The Chavín hegemony seems to have broken up some time
around 500 B.C. Objects in pure Chavín style are not found in
provincial regions after that time, and local styles began to evolve.
The breakdown was not uniform, as some local cultures—such as
Paracas on the south coast—maintained contact with the Chavín
heartland when others had already broken away. On the whole,
however, there was a rapid return to regional cultures and relatively small-scale political organization, in which at most three or
four coastal valleys or half of a large highlands basin were unified
under a single authority. But while Chavín influence died out, the
Rural Nucleated state as a type of of society did not disappear.

Late in the Early Horizon, perhaps around 350 or 400 B.C., a
new kind of society began to grow up in southern Peru, outside of
the area where Rural Nucleated states had developed. This was
the Urban state, in which government, religion, industry, com-

FIGURE 3.3   Nazca trophy head vessel.

merce, and a large population of specialists were concentrated in cities and entered into symbiotic exchanges of goods and services with the farmers living in the hinterlands. The earliest cities known to date were relatively small (perhaps 5,000–10,000 persons) and were located on the southern coast.

The Early Intermediate Period (c. 250 B.C.–A.D. 600) is famous for the great art works that it produced, but it was important too for a number of developments in agriculture, technology, and society. It has been called the "classic" or "florescent" stage of Peruvian civilization. For many societies it was indeed a time of artistic and architectural florescence (see Figures 3.3 and 3.4). Nazca and Moche potters, weavers, and mural painters produced many of the finest masterpieces known from ancient Peru. Most of the adobe pyramids that dot the northern and central coastal valleys—probably thousands in all—were built during the Early Intermediate Period. Metallurgy, which had been invented in the Early Horizon, quickly reached a peak. Copper, gold, and silver were worked by

FIGURE 3.4   Moche portrait head vessel.

smelting, hammering, annealing, cutting, embossing, repoussé, soldering, gilding, casting, and *cire perdue* (lost wax) casting. Most metal artifacts were ornaments, but fishhooks, tweezers, spearthrower hooks, chisels, spear points, and digging stick tips attest to a practical aspect of the craft.

The Early Intermediate Period is marked by a number of interrelated processes that together transformed ancient Peruvian society. The burgeoning population explosion now reached its peak on most of the coast and in parts of the highlands. As the number of people grew toward the limits of the food supplies, new measures were taken to expand farm land and productivity. Greater acreage was devoted to such high-yield crops as maize, manioc, and, for the first time in the known record, potatoes. Small-scale, single-community irrigation had been practiced on the coast since before 1600 B.C., but during the Early Intermediate Period the great valley-wide systems were dug. With all of the rural population organized and all of the water directed into a single comprehensive system, the entire valley bottoms and surrounding slopes could be farmed, and acreage was probably multiplied several times over.

Some basic changes in the distribution of population were apparently also related to the desire to maximize arable land. In northern Peru the old valley-bottom villages were gradually abandoned, and new settlements were strung out along the edges of the valleys on unirrigable desert land. In southern Peru much of the population was concentrated in cities and towns, and a full Synchoritic Urban organization rapidly evolved; that is, a city was associated with a permanent resident rural population in the countryside. Some of the cities, especially in the southern highlands, are among the largest ever built in ancient Peru. Two of them, Huari and Tiahuanaco, were soon to play key roles in the reunification of Peru.

The big irrigation systems, the shifting of settlements, and the vast scale of public construction all imply a ruling class in firm control of each regional state. This inference is confirmed by other lines of evidence, including differentiated settlements and cemeteries and the great volume of regional trade in luxury goods. The most spectacular evidence, however, is found on painted and sculptured Moche pottery from the north coast. Scene after scene shows rulers and priests—often interchangeable with gods—in various relationships to their subjects, seated on thrones or carried in litters, with special clothing, hats, and ornaments to mark their rank.

Still another element of this evolving complex, again related to increasing population pressures on the land, was the rapid upswing of warfare among the regional states. Numerous hilltop fortifications were built; pottery, textiles, and murals depict soldiers, battles, and trophy heads; weapons, trophy heads, and bodies that met violent ends are all common in the cemeteries. There is even some evidence of boundaries shifting by as much as two or three coastal valleys as one or the other of neighboring states achieved military ascendency.

Nor was Peru alone affected by these processes. Agriculture, small-scale irrigation, and settled village life first appeared in north-western Argentina and highland Chile early in the Early Inter-mediate Period. At least on the Ecuadorian coast, if not through-out the northern Andes, a demographic peak was accompanied by unusual prosperity and by some exceptionally large settlements. Though the latter lack the permanent constructions typical of Peru-vian sites, their very size would seem to qualify them as cities of some sort. Especially noteworthy is the Guangala site of La Liber-tad, which was nearly as large as the modern city that stands in its place. At this time, too, the Ecuadorian coast was linked into trade networks that extended southward into Peru, eastward to the Ecua-dorian highlands, and northward probably as far as Costa Rica. This period of prosperity lasted until about A.D. 500.

About A.D. 600 three centers began to expand their spheres of influence. These were Huari in the southern Peruvian highlands, Tiahuanaco in western Bolivia, and Pachacamac on the central Peruvian coast. The Huari expansion took approximately a cen-tury and was clearly brought about through conquest, garrison-ing of conquered territory, and establishment of an empire-wide administrative system. This empire incorporated all of Peru except the southernmost coast and highlands, the *montaña,* and possibly the central coast.

Pachacamac was an important ceremonial center that came to dominate a stretch of about 300 miles of the Peruvian coast. The distribution of Pachacamac sites and art objects does not suggest a conquest empire. Rather, its preeminence probably was due to the prestige of the oracle in the ceremonial center. It is not clear whether Pachacamac territory was entirely independent or whether it was a semi-autonomous province of the Huari empire.

We know almost nothing about the timing and nature of Tia-huanaco expansion. It may have been by conquest in Bolivia and southernmost Peru, but it does not seem to have been so in north-ern Chile. Most major Tiahuanaco sites seem to have been temples rather than lay administrative centers, and the Tiahuanaco expan-sion may have been more like that of Chavín and Pachacamac than that of Huari.

Regardless of the different nature of their expansion, the three centers seem to have been in close contact with one another. Their art styles, especially in pottery, are closely related, and they worshiped the same deities. Both the gods and the basic art style had originated at Tiahuanaco during the Early Intermediate Period and been carried to Huari and Pachacamac at the beginning of the Middle Horizon.

The Huari empire broke up about A.D. 1000, and at about the same time the Tiahuanaco and Pachacamac hegemonies came to an end. We do not know the reasons for this disintegration, but its effects were spectacular. Throughout southern Peru the cities were abandoned. People spread out across the countryside in little villages, and there is some reason to believe that the population may have been considerably reduced. Throughout the Late Intermediate Period (A.D. 1000–1476) southern Peru was basically rural in population distribution and was divided into scores of little warring tribes. Monumental architecture decayed, and almost the only major new public constructions were hilltop fortresses and defensive walls around settlements.

Changes in northern Peru were no less fundamental. With the Huari conquest of that area the old ceremonial centers were abandoned, and much of the population was brought together into cities and towns. Some of the cities seem to have been built for defense against the advancing Huari armies. Others were probably built by order of the Huari governors. Still others may have been initiated by the local nobility in imitation of their conquerors' lifeways. In one way or another, the old Rural Nucleated states were transformed into a Synchoritic Urban organization, at first as provinces of the Huari empire, then, after the fall of Huari, as independent regional states. The Rural type, however, did not evolve into the Urban type but rather was replaced by it as part of the process of building and consolidating an empire.

Just as urbanism passed from southern to northern Peru, so also for a while did the centers of power and the banner of empire. While southern Peru sank into tribalism and internecine warfare, the reestablished regional states of the north prospered. After a few centuries of (probably not very peaceful) coexistence, one of these states set out to reconquer Peru. This was the Chimor empire, with its capital at Chan Chan in the Moche Valley. Between about 1370 and 1465 the Chimor army conquered the coast northward to the modern Peruvian boundary and southward nearly to Lima.

Meanwhile, after about 1438, the Incas of Cuzco emerged as the dominant power in the southern highlands. Probably taking their inspiration from traditions about the Huari empire and from information filtering in from the Chimor empire, they set out to conquer the entire Andean area. By the time their armies met those of Chimor, they were the greatest military power in South America, and the Chimor strongholds seem to have presented little resistance to the Inca steamroller. By 1532, when the Spaniards arrived, the Incas had conquered all of the coast and highlands of modern Ecuador, Peru, Bolivia, northwestern Argentina, and northern Chile. Furthermore, in less than a century, they had organized all of this territory into a monolithic state with a central government whose efficiency was a source of constant astonishment to the Spanish conquerors.

The Incas made no especially significant contributions to ancient Peruvian technology or food production. Their special genius, which enabled them to conquer and hold most of western South America, was as military strategists, diplomats, and administrators. Many areas were taken, not by the army, but by submission to the threats of ambassadors. Uprisings were, of course, put down by the military, but several policies (including the large-scale shifting of population from one province to another) tended to keep revolts from developing. Local rulers and gods were incorporated into the hierarchy. The whole empire was linked by an integrated highway system. The Incas increased the production of bronze tools and made them available to ordinary farmers. Taxes were collected primarily in labor. Without a written language, the Incas kept a constantly up-to-date census of the population and economic resources of their empire.

One of the most striking features of the Inca empire is that it was not based on an urban organization. Centered as it was in the ruralized southern highlands, its whole organization was rural in concept and practice. Cuzco was little more than a cluster of villages when the Inca expansion began and was rebuilt into something resembling more a ceremonial center than a city. Most of the northern cities were largely abandoned after the Inca conquest. The new rulers seldom built a settlement of more than about 1,000 persons, even when they were concentrating a scattered population to increase their control over it. Even administrative centers, garrisons, storehouses, and government road houses were often built in the countryside rather than in populated centers.

There is some reason to believe that the Incas, in spite of their administrative talents and their improved facilities for transportation and communication, may have overextended themselves in conquering so much territory. The six-year Spanish conquest of their empire was not due to any marked European military superiority. Rather, Pizarro and his men arrived toward the end of a disastrous civil war between rival aspirants to the throne, one seated in Cuzco, the other in Quito. The Spanish were able to take advantage not only of the rancors created by civil strife, but also of the rebellious spirit of provincial peoples whose desire for independence had been nurtured by the internal strife between Inca factions. The Incas, in short, may have suffered from demographic and territorial indigestion.

· BIBLIOGRAPHIC ESSAY

There are four general summaries of Peruvian prehistory. The first of them, by Wendell Bennett and Junius Bird, is *Andean Culture History,* Handbook Series, No. 15 (New York: American Museum of Natural History, 1949). Based primarily on data from the Virú Valley, it begins with the late preceramic and organizes its material in developmental stages. The section by Bird, "Technology," is an excellent summary of the way ancient pottery, textiles, metalwork, etc. were made. J. Alden Mason's book *The Ancient Civilizations of Peru* (Harmondsworth, Middlesex: Pelican Books, A395, 1957) is noteworthy for its extensive description of the social, political, and religious organization of the Inca empire, as well as for its descriptive treatment of Peruvian prehistory. Another and more up-to-date source on the latter subject, again organized in developmental stages based on the Virú Valley, is G. H. S. Bushnell's *Peru,* Ancient Peoples and Places Series (London: Thames and Hudson, 1956). For a different approach, based on time periods rather than stages, see Edward P. Lanning's *Peru Before the Incas* (Englewood Cliffs, N.J.: Prentice-Hall, 1967). Perhaps the definitive study of the Inca empire is the long article by John H. Rowe, "Inca Culture at the Time of the Spanish Conquest," in the *Handbook of South American Indians*, Vol. 2, Smithsonian Institution, Bureau of American Ethnology, Bulletin 143 (1946). Settlement pattern studies, of overwhelming importance to Peruvianists, were initiated by Gordon Willey in his book *Prehistoric Settlement Patterns in the Virú Valley*, Smithsonian Institution, Bureau of American Ethnology, Bulletin 155 (1953), which continues to be the fullest and most complete work of this sort done for Peru.

Ecuador and Colombia are best appreciated by reading *Ecuador* by Betty J. Meggers (New York: Praeger, 1966) and *Colombia* by Gerardo Reichel-Dolmatoff (New York: Praeger, 1965). Meggers' book is primarily descriptive and involves a great deal of inevitable guess-dating of which the reader should beware. Reichel-Dolmatoff's book, on the other hand, presents and illustrates a general theory on the nature and causes of the development of the ancient cultures of that country.

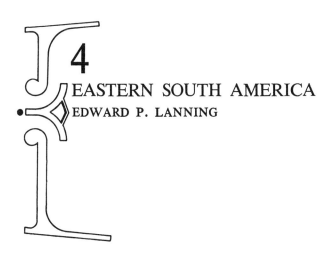

4
EASTERN SOUTH AMERICA
EDWARD P. LANNING

By "eastern South America" we mean that vast part of the continent that lies to the east of the Andean mountain chain (Map 4.1). It is drained by three great river systems, which separate two areas of ancient, heavily eroded mountains from each other and from the flatlands of eastern Patagonia. Comprising as it does the larger part of an entire continent, eastern South America includes a great variety of different climates and environments.

Fully two-thirds of the land mass lies within the tropics. This area includes the northern coast of Venezuela, the Orinoco and Amazon basins, the Guiana highlands, and most of the Brazilian highlands. This is hot country. Except for parts of the Venezuelan coast and of northeastern Brazil, it receives heavy rainfall. The river basins are largely covered by dense tropical rain forest, the highlands by grassy savannahs or scrub forest, the coasts by forests and mangrove swamps. In the river basins, which were the focus of human population, settlements and farm lands were and are located primarily on river banks and islands, and transportation was principally by canoe along the waterways. In general, this tropical area is one of low terrestrial biomass and poor wild food resources, though fish are abundant in the streams and rivers. Swidden farming with manioc as the staple was the primary source of food in the forested basins. Wild foods were somewhat more abundant and more important in the human diet in the drier highlands zones.

To the south of the tropical area lie the La Plata basin and the

MAP 4.1   Archaeological sites in eastern South America.

flatlands of the Gran Chaco, the pampas, and Patagonia. Rainfall is less here and, except in the Gran Chaco, temperatures cooler. The La Plata basin and surrounding country are covered with grass—the famous pampas of Argentina, Uruguay, and southern Brazil. The area to the east and south of the pampas, including the entire Patagonian plateau, consists of semi-arid scrub steppe. On the whole, this southern third of the continent was not propitious for native farming, in some areas because of its aridity and (in Patagonia) extreme cold, in others because the Indians could not easily clear grasslands with wooden tools. Though some farming was practiced everywhere that the climate permitted, hunting and gathering were of more importance than they were in Amazonia and the Orinoco. The principal game animal was the guanaco, which roamed the area in great herds.

At its southern tip South America is fringed by rocky islands and capped off by Tierra del Fuego. These islands, which represent the southern portion of the south Chilean archipelago, would seem most inhospitable places for man. Subarctic in climate, they (like the adjacent Patagonian mainland) offer no possibility of farming, nor are they rich in land fauna or in edible plant foods. They do, however, provide a rich harvest of fish, shellfish, sea lions, and other marine resources. The "Canoe Indians" who occupied them lived primarily off these resources.

Archaeological research in eastern South America has been sporadic and of widely differing quality. For some areas, such as coastal Venezuela, the Orinoco Basin, and the Ucayali River, intensive research has produced good chronologies, but there is little information on subjects other than ceramics. For others, such as the Amazon Basin, only a few small, widely separated zones in a vast area have been studied at all, and these studies have led to almost irresoluble conflicts in interpretation. Elsewhere, as in central and northern Patagonia, a good deal of research seems to have produced little that can be fit into any kind of systematic framework. In short, to attempt to make sense out of the prehistory of lowlands South America is rather like trying to articulate a jigsaw puzzle from which 95 percent of the pieces are missing. Prudence requires the examination of major areas separately rather than a synthesis of the entire area. Chart 4.1 should help the reader to relate the various cultures to one another.

	UCAYALI RIVER	MARAJO ISLAND	LOWER ORINOCO	CENTRAL VENEZUELA COAST	EASTERN VENEZUELA COAST	CUBA
1500 A.D.	Caimito	Marajoara	El Morro	Cumarego	Punta Arenas	Pueblo Viejo
1000 A.D.	Cumancaya					
	Nueva Esperanza					Cayo Redondo
500 A.D.	Cashibocaño	Acauan	Barrancos			
	Pacacocha					
	Yarinacocha					
1		Formiga			Punta Gorda	
	Hupa-Iya		Barrancas			Guayabo Blanco
500 B.C.	Late Shakimu	Mangueiras				
	Early Shakimu					
1000		Anariatuba	Saladero	Iguanas		
	Late Tutishcainyo				Manicuare	
2000	Early Tutishcainyo					
3000				Heneal		
4000					Cubagua	
5000						
6000						
7000						
8000						

CHART 4.1   Phases of eastern South American culture.

HISPANIOLA	EAST BRAZIL HIGHLANDS	SOUTH BRAZIL COAST	BUENOS AIRES	NORTH PATAGONIA	SOUTH PATAGONIA	SOUTH ARCHIPELAGO
Carrier	Taguara	Ilha dos Ratos	Bolívar		Magellan V	Beagle Channel II
Meillac Macady Couri	Guatambu			Tehuelche II	Magellan IV	Beagle Channel I
Cabaret	Cara		Claromeío	Tehuelche I		
Mordan	Umbu / Paiqueré	Macedo / Saquarema / Gomes	Blanco Grande	Proto-Tehuelche	Magellan III	Englefield Island
Casimira	Antas		Tandilia			
	Cerca Grande			San Jorge / Jacobacce	Magellan II	
				Río Gallegos		

· THE AMAZON AND ORINOCO BASINS

The vast river systems of the Amazon and Orinoco contain the bulk of South America's tropical rain forest. No archaeological sites older than *c.* 2000 B.C. have yet been found in this vast territory, and there are probably several reasons for this lack of early sites. Silting and river-bank cutting bury or destroy sites, and older sites have correspondingly less chance of survival. Dense vegetation makes surface survey impossible, so that sites can be found only along recent or modern river courses. Above all, earlier populations were probably small and thinly scattered, because the environment is at best unfavorable for hunters and gatherers.

The most intensive studies have been made on the Middle Ucayali River in Peru, at the mouth of the Amazon, and in the lower Orinoco Basin in both Venezuela and Guyana. Less complete information is available for a few points on each river and its tributaries. In spite of the paucity of research in such a vast area, certain features of the archaeological record stand out as significant. From the beginning, almost all of the archaeological sites represent sedentary villages occupied for some length of time. There are neither the camp sites expected of food gatherers, nor the diversity of environmentally specialized locales found in such areas as the Andes. The tropical forest pattern of achoritic village life based on swidden farming ("achoritic" implying that the farmers lived in the villages rather than in the hinterland) had apparently been established by 2000 B.C. and remained stable thereafter.

Another prominent characteristic is the wide dispersal of certain ceramic traditions. Pottery styles from points throughout both river systems are often so similar that they must be historically related to one another and derived from a single source. This phenomenon is unquestionably a function of canoe travel on the long, interconnected waterways of Amazonia and the Orinoco. Travel was faster and easier on these rivers than anywhere else on the continent.

While there is general agreement that the wide distribution of ceramic traditions represents rapid movement of peoples by canoe, there is controversy over the identification of these peoples and over the direction of the movements. Some authorities maintain that each ceramic tradition is the product of peoples of a single linguistic stock; others hold that there is no necessary connection between ceramic styles and language families. I can see no resolution to the problem at this time.

Again, there are two contradictory theories as to the origins of the ceramic traditions. One is that their diffusion represents the spread of peoples out of the Andes down into the tropical forest. The other is that it is a product of migrations of tropical forest peoples out of the central portions of the major rivers. The latter, espoused by Donald Lathrap for the Amazon and (to a lesser degree) by Irving Rouse and José Cruxent for the Orinoco, fits the facts far better than the former, and I believe that it is true in most cases. It is supported by distributional and chronological evidence within the tropical forest and by the fact that these traditions are never found in the Andes proper but only on their forested eastern slopes. Then, too, it is precisely in the great river valleys of the tropical forest that we would expect population pressure to build up to the point of forcing frequent and massive population movements. The scarcity of good farmland and of protein resources, the impossibility of maintaining dense populations without spreading out, the open frontiers, and the ease of transportation, all argue for lowland sources of migration. In addition, such migrations continued during the historic period. Three major linguistic stocks were spread over much of the tropical forest by this means. The Arawakan migrations were apparently finished by the time the Spaniards and Portuguese arrived, but those of the Tupian and Cariban peoples were still in process. None of them had an Andean point of origin.

The earliest of the known tropical forest cultures are Tutishcainyo (*c.* 2000–1000 B.C.) on the Middle Ucayali and Saladero (*c.* 1000–800 B.C.) on the Lower Orinoco. Both are characterized by substantial refuse deposits yielding well-made pottery in which carinated and base-angled bowls are the dominant forms. Tutishcainyo pottery is primarily incised (Figure 4.1), Saladero pottery mainly painted with red and white-on-red designs (Figure 4.2). Both wares show a high degree of skill in their manufacture. Neither is remotely similar to what one might expect of a recently invented craft. Nor are they similar to the earlier pottery from Puerto

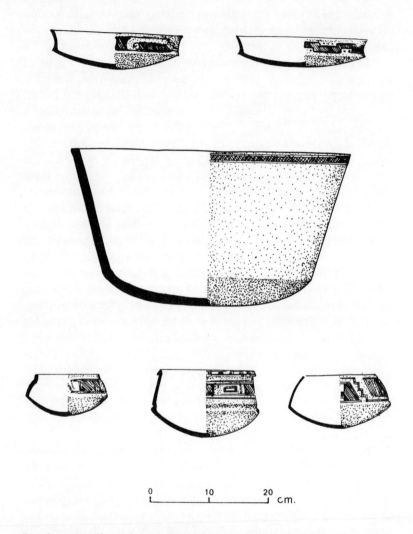

```
0        10        20
|____|____|____|____| cm.
```

Based on an illustration in Donald Lathrap, *The Upper Amazon* (New York: Praeger, 1970; London: Thames and Hudson, 1970).

FIGURE 4.1   Tutishcainyo pottery.

Adapted with permission from *Arqueología Cronológica de Venezuela,* Vol. 2, by J. M. Cruxent and I. Rouse (Washington, D.C.: Organization of American States, 1961).

FIGURE 4.2   Sherds of the Saladero style.

Hormiga (3100 B.C.) and Valdívia (2800 B.C.) on the coasts of Colombia and Ecuador. There must have been a long tradition of pottery-making behind them, and we may reasonably expect to find earlier pottery in the tropical forest when the area has been better studied.

That the Tutishcainyo and Saladero peoples were farmers is almost certain, since food gatherers would not have left such large, substantial refuse deposits in the tropical forest environment. In all likelihood the main staple was manioc, with fish as the principal source of protein, just as it was in later times. Griddles for the baking of bread from bitter manioc have been found at Saladero, and fish bones and scales got mixed into the clay from which Tutishcainyo pottery was made. The griddles today are used for making bread of bitter (poisonous) manioc. Sweet manioc, which is simply boiled or roasted, may have been in use at a much earlier time, since it had diffused all the way to the Peruvian coast before 1000 B.C. The griddles, too, have appeared in the Venezuelan Andes far back in the second millennium B.C., and bitter manioc should be even older somewhere in the tropical forest.

After about 500 B.C., Saladero-like pottery is found in sites all along the Orinoco and on the Venezuelan coast, and it soon spread throughout the Caribbean islands. The Tutishcainyo tradition, insofar as it is now known, developed locally through the Shakimu style until about 200 B.C., apparently with frequent interchange of stylistic ideas between the potters of the Middle Ucayali and those of the Peruvian highlands.

The first ceramic tradition to spread widely across both the Amazon and Orinoco basins, as well as the Venezuelan coast, was that known as Barrancoid. This tradition includes many local ceramic styles with very similar vessel shapes, decorated by incision and with a great variety of incised and anthropomorphic lugs and adornos. Bitter-manioc griddles occur in large quantities, as do large urn-like vessels presumed to be containers for manioc beer. Spindle whorls, suggesting the weaving of cotton cloth, appear for the first time, as do tobacco pipes. (See Figure 4.3.)

The earliest known occurrence of the Barrancoid tradition is on the Lower Orinoco, where the Barrancas style appears at about 800 B.C. The style is intrusive in the area, abruptly replacing the

Adapted with permission from *Arqueología Cronológica de Venezuela,* Vol. 2, by J. M. Cruxent and I. Rouse (Washington, D.C.: Organization of American States, 1961).

FIGURE 4.3   Barrancoid artifacts.

older Saladero style, and is thought to have come from the Upper Orinoco or the Middle Amazon. Unfortunately, the Barrancoid sites in those areas either have not been dated or else represent relatively late manifestations of the traditions. The Ucayali seems clearly not to have been its source, since it did not appear there until about 200 B.C., when the Hupa-Iya complex replaced the native Shakimu culture.

The Barrancoid tradition was undoubtedly spread by canoe travel along the major waterways of the Amazon and Orinoco systems. While part of this spread may have been by simple diffusion of stylistic modes from one settlement to another, it is likely that much of it was due to a major wave of migration like those which, in historic times, led to the displacement of native peoples as powerful tribes spread out. Donald Lathrap has suggested that this tradition was carried by the speakers of one group (Maipuran) of the Arawakan languages, within whose historic territory many of the archaeological sites are found.

The Barrancoid tradition proper lasted until about 500 B.C. in the Amazon Basin. It was succeeded by (and partly contemporaneous with) a great many cultures whose pottery shows a bewildering diversity of style and complexity of interrelationships. A very large number of the new ceramic styles feature incised and polychrome painted designs based on scroll and step designs, and (locally) combed or corrugated surfaces. The practice of burial in large urns appears to be universal among these cultural complexes. Lathrap has proposed a three-part subdivision of these styles:

1. A Guarita sub-tradition, evolved out of the Barrancoid tradition after 500 B.C., presumably representing the descendants of the peoples who made Barrancoid pottery.
2. A Miracanguera sub-tradition including, among others, Caimito on the Middle Ucayali, Napo on the Napo River in Ecuador, and Marajoara on Marajó Island at the mouth of the Amazon. He proposes that this tradition, which spread some time after 1000 B.C., represents the remains of Tupian peoples. (See Figure 4.4.)
3. The Cumancaya style of the Middle Ucayali, derived from eastern Bolivia and made by Panoan-speaking peoples.

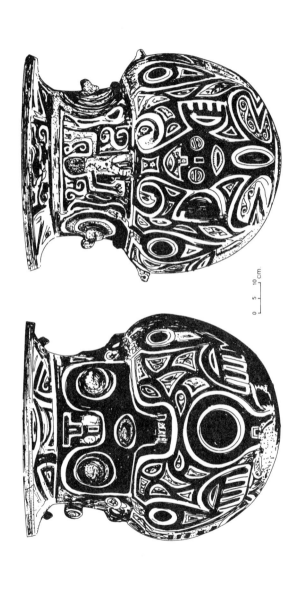

Based on an illustration in B. J. Meggers and C. Evans, *Archeological Investigations at the Mouth of the Amazon* (Washington, D.C.: Smithsonian Institution, Bureau of American Ethnology, Bulletin 167, 1957).

0 5 10 cm

FIGURE 4.4   Marajoara phase burial urn.

I am not convinced by the Bolivian derivation of Cumancaya, but the evidence supporting the Miracangueran association with Tupians and the Cumancaya association with Panoans is impressive, since both traditions have continued in modified form to the present day and are the products, respectively, of Tupian-speaking and Panoan-speaking peoples.

On the Orinoco, the Barrancoid tradition lasted until about A.D. 1000 and was then replaced mainly by the Arauquinoid tradition. The latter is characterized by incised designs, usually in the form of bands of triangles, and by appliqué decoration and modeled heads. It has been suggested that this tradition, together with certain late styles from the Amazon Basin featuring bands of incised triangles, represents the remains of the Cariban-speaking peoples. I find this attribution doubtful. Almost all of these styles in both river basins are found outside of the territory of the historic Caribs and within the territory of historic Arawakan peoples.

The last major expansion in the tropical forest was that of the Cariban peoples, which was being vigorously carried out when Europeans arrived in the area. Yet there seems to be no unified stylistic tradition in the Amazon and Orinoco basins to mark their presence. Lathrap has proposed an ingenious explanation for such a lack:

> . . . it was raiding parties of young men who attacked the neighboring peoples. All adult males of the conquered villages were barbecued and eaten while the more desirable women were taken as wives.
>
> If it is correct to assume that art style and ceramic technology were feminine domains, it would be predictable that these patterns would be transmitted in a poorly understood and garbled form, since there would be few, if any, properly trained women moving out of the old Carib hearth-land.*

In other words, Carib women stayed home; Carib men took over new territory, women and all; and these women continued to make pottery largely in their own native tradition. Small wonder that there is no unified Carib style.

* Donald Lathrap, *The Upper Amazon* (New York: Praeger, 1970), pp. 164–165.

· THE CARIBBEAN

The Caribbean area, as defined here, includes the islands of the Caribbean Sea and the coast of central and eastern Venezuela and the Guianas. The islands are logically included in a consideration of eastern South American prehistory, since there is ample evidence that almost all of their historic Indian population came originally from South America, displacing peoples who had moved into the area from Central America and possibly Florida.

Conditions were much more favorable for hunting and gathering peoples in the Caribbean area than in the tropical forests of the mainland. This was especially true along the coastlines of both the mainland and the islands, where the ocean provided ample subsistence. At the same time, old archaeological sites stand in little danger of being destroyed and are fairly easy to find. Not surprisingly, the archaeological record goes back farther in time than that of Amazonia and the Orinoco. As far as the islands are concerned, the earliest known archaeological sites are probably very close in time to the dates of first settlement—i.e., to the time when continental peoples developed canoes and moved out into the Caribbean Sea.

The central coast of Venezuela was occupied by food gatherers by about 4000 B.C., its eastern coast by about 3000 B.C. The most characteristic artifact of the Heneal complex of the central coast is an edge-ground stone also found in the preceramic of Panama. The Cubagua and Manicuare complexes of the eastern coast are known for their variety of bone and shell artifacts, including (in Manicuare) the shell gouges used to make dugout canoes. In both areas, the archaeological sites are deep, substantial shellmounds that suggest permanent and fairly sedentary village life on the shore. These eastern coastal cultures reached some of the offshore islands but did not penetrate into the Antilles.

Cuba and Hispaniola—the two largest islands—were occupied by the third millennium B.C., if not somewhat earlier. The Guayabo Blanco complex of Cuba includes shell gouges and other artifacts suggestive of Manicuare, but the same artifact types are known from the preceramic of Florida. The proximity of Cuba to the Florida coast, and the absence of similar artifacts on the islands between it and Venezuela, has led to the hypothesis that Cuba was first inhabited by Indians from Florida some time during the third millennium B.C. On Hispaniola, the Casimira and Mordan complexes are characterized by flint blades of types that suggest Central American ancestry. On other islands, such as Trinidad and Puerto Rico, there is no evidence of human occupation until nearly the time of Christ. As elsewhere in the area, the earliest sites here are coastal shellmounds without evidence of farming. Except for the edge-grinders characteristic of Heneal, they show no special affinities to continental South American cultures.

It thus appears that the entire Caribbean area was first occupied by food gatherers who lived on the shore and ate primarily fish and shellfish. They filtered out onto the islands at different times and from different places in North, Central, and South America, bringing with them very different material cultures.

Early in the Christian era, pottery of the Saladoid tradition spread along the eastern coast of Venezuela and out into the Caribbean as far as Puerto Rico. Abundant clay griddles give evidence that the cultivation of bitter manioc spread along with the pottery. There is every reason to believe that this phenomenon represents the migration of manioc farmers out of the Orinoco Basin, and that these new immigrants displaced or killed off the resident gathering peoples. They were almost certainly speakers of the Arawakan languages that ultimately spread throughout the Caribbean area, because there is no other time in the area's prehistory when South American cultures penetrated beyond Trinidad.

The subsequent culture history of the Caribbean area is varied. Along most of the Venezuelan and Guianan coasts the pattern of manioc-based village life, without marked evidence of ceremonialism, remained constant. At Cerro Machado on the central coast, however, there was a brief intrusion of Andean influences about the time of Christ. The pottery was decorated in a style derived from the Venezuelan Andes, and the lack of manioc griddles suggests that maize had temporarily become the staple crop. At Lake Valencia, again in north-central Venezuela, the appearance, about A.D. 1000, of urn burials and of artificial mounds as substructures for houses suggests influences from the Upper Orinoco.

In the Antilles, three strongly marked tendencies are to be seen.

One is the continued spread of ceramics, manioc farming, and (presumably) Arawakan languages at the expense of the older food-gathering, aceramic way of life. The farming peoples gradually moved westward to Hispaniola, Jamaica, and Cuba. They did not, however, completely replace the food gatherers, some of whom (the Ciboney) still occupied unfavorable parts of Cuba and Hispaniola when the Spaniards arrived in 1492. A second trend, clearly related to the spread of agriculture, was the gradual filling up of the interiors of the larger islands by people moving in from the coast.

The third major development seems to have been the result of contact with the peoples of Mesoamerica. Starting shortly before A.D. 1000, the Taino peoples of Puerto Rico, Hispaniola, and eastern Cuba developed an elaborate ceremonial life centered on certain deities called *zemis*. The material remains of these ceremonies include ball courts and dance plazas with stone walls, large stone idols, and a variety of special small stone artifacts. The ball courts and plazas are so characteristic of Mesoamerica that they must have diffused from there. These islands, however, were never part of the Mesoamerican empires, nor were they invaded or occupied by people from Mesoamerica.

One final development in Caribbean prehistory is not obvious in the archaeological record. By the time Europeans arrived, the lesser Antilles were in the hands of the ferocious and rapidly expanding Caribs. As we have seen, these people seem not to have left the material remains of a unified cultural tradition, but their presence is attested by the writings of the early European conquerors.

· THE EASTERN BRAZILIAN HIGHLANDS

Some of the most famous and controversial archaeological sites in eastern South America are caves in the Lagoa Santa region of Minas Gerais. Since early in the nineteenth century it has been claimed that man there was contemporary with extinct Pleistocene animals; indeed, the skeletons from these caves have been used to define an archetypal race of very ancient Americans. This "Lagoa

Santa race" is no longer believed to be different from other South American Indians, and recent excavations have failed to support the contention that the caves were occupied during the Pleistocene. The only dated and well-defined culture is the Cerca Grande complex, which includes square-stemmed and barbed projectile points, spokeshaves, a variety of scrapers, percussion-flaked choppers, and semi-polished stone axes, as well as bone projectile points, awls, and beads, and shell beads. One Cerca Grande site has been radiocarbon-dated to the eighth millennium B.C., but the culture may have endured until a much more recent date. Pottery was eventually introduced to the area, but its age and affiliations are unknown.

There are several partial sequences for Brazil's southernmost state, Rio Grande do Sul. The most complete one, shown in composite form in Chart 4.1, is fairly typical of most of the area. Lithic industries of choppers, scrapers, and a variety of rough flake tools are widespread throughout inland southern Brazil. Several radiocarbon dates place them in the period 5000–2000 B.C. (Antas and Paiqueré complexes). Stemmed and lanceolate projectile points, the former said to resemble Magellan IV forms, first appear in the Umbu complex (4000–2300 B.C.). Shell fishhooks and bone projectile points are also found here. Hereafter there is a marked distinction between hunting sites and food-gathering sites, but it is not clear whether these represent different cultures or only seasonally different camps of the same people. Polished and semi-polished stone axes appear in these assemblages at a relatively late date, probably c. 2000 B.C. in the Camboatá complex. Pottery does not appear until around 300 or 400 B.C.

The southern Brazilian coast is known for its massive shellmounds, or *sambaquís,* which lie along the edges of ancient and modern mangrove swamps. Research on these middens is recent and only partially published. The best known are those from the state of Paraná. Here the preceramic sites contain assemblages dominated by stone axes, choppers, and scrapers, together with a few projectile points. In the Sambaquí do Gomes (3000–2500 B.C.) and the lower levels of the Sambaquí do Saquarema (2300–1900 B.C.) the axes are all percussion-flaked and the projectile points are stemmed forms of stone. In the upper levels of Saquarema and in the Sambaquí do Macedo (1650–1300 B.C.) many of the axes are semi-polished, and in Macedo bone projectile points replace the stone forms. The only dated pottery in Paraná is from the Sambaquí da Ilha dos Ratos (A.D. 1450). Pottery is generally assumed to have appeared late in this area, but the actual time of its introduction is not known.

The abundance of stone axes at an early date in eastern Brazil is of considerable interest. Such tools are usually associated with the clearing of land for planting. If they were so used in this case, cultivation (presumably of manioc) must go back to the very beginning of the Holocene. It is possible, though, that on this early time level the axes were used only to fell trees for houses and canoes.

· THE PAMPAS AND PATAGONIA

The northernmost place in Argentina—and the only place in the Argentine pampas—for which there are reliable stratigraphic sequences is in the province of Buenos Aires, near the mouth of the Paraná River. Rather than treat the Paraná Basin and the pampas separately, it is convenient to discuss these sequences along with those of Patagonia.

Patagonian archaeology is not easy to either summarize or synthesize. There is one reasonably complete stratigraphic sequence from the Straits of Magellan in the south, and there are shorter, partial sequences, from Tierra del Fuego and the province of Buenos Aires. There are few radiocarbon dates for the entire area. Worse, there is a vast and confusing multiplicity of named cultural complexes, almost none of them described or even illustrated in the literature. Some of the names apply to what seem to be identical assemblages found in different geographical contexts and ascribed to widely differing ages. Others almost certainly represent different seasonal aspects of a single cultural complex carried by a single people. Wherever the name of a well-known "culture" is lacking from Chart 4.1, it is because of the suspicion or certainty that it represents the same people and complex as one that appears on the chart. Also, the scarcity of stratigraphy and radiocarbon dates means that a great deal of guesswork has gone into the corresponding columns of the chart.

The area may be divided into four sections, each of which seems to show reasonable internal cultural homogeneity at any given time, and each of which differs in significant ways from the others. These are the pampas; northern Patagonia from the Río Negro to the Río Chico; southern Patagonia from the Río Chico to the Straits of Magellan; and Tierra del Fuego and the southern Chilean archipelago. Maize and calabashes were grown around the Paraná delta at the northern end of the pampas; otherwise the entire area was occupied by guanaco hunters and, on the shores and in the archipelago, fishermen and hunters of sea mammals.

Buenos Aires archaeology is characterized throughout by a lithic industry dominated by side and end scrapers and a variety of other unifacially and unilaterally chipped tools. Side scrapers are most abundant at the beginning of the sequence, end scrapers in its later phases. The preceramic complexes (Tandilia I through Montura) show a progressive refinement of stone-chipping technique. Triangular projectile points and simple pottery appear in the inland Archaic Bolívar and coastal Early Bonairense complexes. This is followed by a period of incised and painted pottery (Recent Bolívar and Classic Bonairense) and finally by the pottery of the historic Guaraní (Late Bonairense) and Araucanian (Epigonal Bolívar) Indians.

The coast of northern Patagonia is characterized by a series of basalt industries—all said to be of quite recent date—featuring such artifacts as little choppers and square, sharp-edged bipolar pieces. Since these types occur in small quantities at inland sites, I suspect that the coastal sites are either lithic quarries used by the inland peoples or seasonal fishing camps of the same peoples. They are therefore not listed separately in Chart 4.1. The post-Pleistocene sequence begins with the Río Gallegos complex, which is characterized by large side scrapers and choppers, the latter apparently present at open sites and not in caves. The succeeding coastal San Jorge and inland Jacobacce complexes, while they contain a few large side scrapers, consist primarily of thick, flat, percussion-flaked bifaces of all sizes, a few of which might have served as rough projectile points. Coastal sites consist of shellmounds made up almost exclusively of *Venus* shells. The bifaces and *Venus*-shell middens continue into Proto-Tehuelche, when pressure flaking reappears for the first time since the Pleistocene, accompanied by triangular projectile points with rounded bases. Tehuelche is characterized by stemmed, concave-based projectile points and a well-developed blade industry including many scrapers made on the ends of blades. Pottery first appears in Tehuelche II, while the reduction in the size of Tehuelche III projectile points suggests the introduction of the bow and arrow. Tehuelche coastal middens are made up primarily of *Mytilus* shells.

The one long, reasonably complete stratigraphic sequence comes from three caves on the Straits of Magellan in southern Patagonia —Fell's, Palli Aike, and Cañadon Leona. The earliest complex, Magellan I, dates to the Late Pleistocene and is therefore not shown in Chart 4.1. It consists of an assemblage dominated by large side scrapers and by fluted fishtail projectile points, associated with the bones of extinct horses and ground sloths. The side scrapers continue to dominate Magellan II, but bone projectile points replace those made of stone. Except for these bone points and for the choppers found at open sites, there is little difference between Magellan II and Río Gallegos. Indeed, Magellan II may be but a seasonal cave-dwelling manifestation of the Río Gallegos complex. In Magellan III we find grooved bolas stones, triangular projectile points, and the same side scrapers as the dominant elements. The bolas stones continue to the end of the sequence. Magellan IV, with its stemmed, concave-based projectile points, looks much like Tehuelche I-II, but it substitutes thumbnail scrapers for the Tehuelche end-of-blade scrapers and lacks the pottery of Tehuelche II. Magellan V is essentially the same industry except that, as in northern Patagonia, a marked decrease in the size of projectile points probably signals the introduction of the bow and arrow.

The southern archipelago is less well-known archaeologically than Patagonia, and its known prehistory does not extend so far into the past. All of the remains can be attributed to the Canoe Indians, who, during historic times, fished and hunted sea mammals among the islands and along the shores of Tierra del Fuego. Englefield Island has, among a welter of unusual and/or idiosyncratic artifacts, a combination of round-based triangular projectile points like those of Proto-Tehuelche and bone harpoons and fish spears much like those of the succeeding archipelago complexes. In Beagle Channel I we find mussel-shell knives, harpoon points and other bone artifacts, bolas stones, and thumbnail scrapers, but no pressure flaking or stone projectile points. Beagle Channel II, attributable to the historic Yahgan, differs primarily in containing a variety of relatively large stemmed and triangular projectile points, none of which look particularly like mainland forms.

The archaeology of the pampas and Patagonia bears out the historic distinction between the Foot Indians—mainland hunters and gatherers—and the Canoe Indians of the archipelago. The large number of relatively recent assemblages without stone projectile points is most unusual for hunting peoples; probably projectiles were tipped by wood or bone, as in Magellan II, for projectiles there must have been. Apart from the reintroduction of the stone projectile point, the appearance of the bolas, and the disappearance of large side scrapers, cultural change as evidenced in the archaeological record seems to have been mostly a matter of stylistic change rather than of change in basic lifeways.

· BIBLIOGRAPHIC ESSAY

The best single book on eastern South America is Donald Lathrap's *The Upper Amazon* (New York: Praeger, 1970). Apart from synthesizing the prehistory of the area indicated by its title, it relates the Upper Amazonian sequences to those of all of Amazonia and of the Orinoco Basin. The latter area, as well as the Caribbean coast, are well described by Irving Rouse and J. M. Cruxent in *Venezuelan Archaeology* (New Haven: Yale University Caribbean Series, No. 6, 1963). Three important primary sources by Clifford Evans and Betty J. Meggers are *Archeological Investigations at the Mouth of the Amazon*, Smithsonian Institution, Bureau of American Ethnology, Bulletin 167 (1957); *Archeological Investigations in British Guiana*, Smithsonian Institution, Bureau of American Ethnology, Bulletin 177 (1960); and *Archeological Investigations on the Río Napo, Eastern Ecuador*, Smithsonian Contributions to Anthropology, Vol. 6 (1968).

The archaeology of the southern half of the area is represented by thousands of articles and books, most of them in Spanish or Portuguese and published in journals not generally available to the public. One extremely important article can be cited, however, since it contains the basic stratigraphic sequence on which almost all Patagonian archaeology is based. This is Junius Bird's "The Archaeology of Patagonia" in the *Handbook of South American Indians,* Vol. 1, Smithsonian Institution, Bureau of American Ethnology, Bulletin 143 (1946).

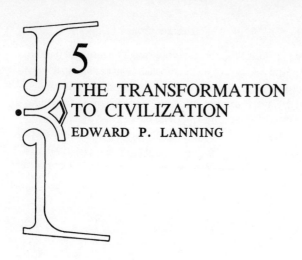

5
THE TRANSFORMATION TO CIVILIZATION
EDWARD P. LANNING

The kinds of societies that archaeologists call "civilizations" grew up in Mesoamerica and in the central Andes. If we want to understand the origins of civilization in the Americas, the best way is to inquire into the historical processes that took place in both of these areas but not elsewhere, where civilizations did not develop.

Before we do so, a definition of "civilization" is in order. Definitions based only on the nature of the Old World civilizations have stressed such accomplishments as writing and metallurgy. These criteria are obviously meaningless in the New World, where the Inca empire was founded and run without the benefit of written records, and that of Teotihuacán thrived without metal tools. They are also irrelevant because nowadays when we talk about "civilization," we are referring primarily to the way a society is organized rather than to its technical accomplishments.

Perhaps no two archaeologists will ever agree entirely on a definition. Looking at the societies to which the name is usually applied, however, we can see that they have certain features in common. All of them have been based on intensive agricultural economies. All of them have had relatively large and densely concentrated populations. Intensive social stratification and occupational specialization, intercommunity patterns of authority, centralization of power, statewide organization of food production, far-ranging distributive systems for both basic goods and luxury

110

products, and intensely diversified settlement patterns are found normally in civilizations, seldom in other kinds of societies.

Most of these features can, under favorable circumstances, leave their mark on the archaeological record. Intensive agriculture can be detected, not only by the quantity and variety of remains of crop plants in dry refuse deposits, but also by the preservation of ancient irrigation systems, terraces, and field boundaries. There are many techniques for making rough estimates of population levels at different periods. True social stratification, based on differential rights of access to resources, can be distinguished from rank systems, which do not necessarily have an economic basis, by an examination of settlements and cemeteries for luxury goods, architectural excellence, and the like. Monumental public constructions that required the joint labor of many communities surely suggest broad patterns of authority based on state, rather than local, autonomy. Distributive systems are best traced through the identification of luxury goods, which in turn can be used to measure the degree of interconnection between geographically separated enclaves of the wealthy or ruling classes. The diversification of settlement patterns is obvious to any archaeologist who has ever conducted a surface survey of sites of a time and place where civilization prevailed.

Under unfavorable circumstances, of course, evidence of these sorts may be destroyed, or the people of a given civilization may never have created it. Ancient irrigation ditches, for example, are fragile things easily eradicated by subsequent plowing, construction, erosion, or alluviation. Again, a society that by other measures was a civilization may have foregone the monumental and permanent in its architecture, building everything of wood which has not survived the ravages of time. The Chibchas of Colombia and the Guangala people of coastal Ecuador may have evolved civilizations that have gone unappreciated for just such reasons. If so, however, their way of life was fundamentally different from that of the ancient Peruvians and Mesoamericans—i.e., they developed a different *kind* of civilization. Our inquiry, then, should be hedged with caution. To rephrase the question posed above: What historical processes took place in Mesoamerica and the central Andes that led to the evolution of the kinds of civilizations found there but did not take place elsewhere where those particular types of society did not evolve?

As we look at settlement patterns, most of the "civilized" societies of Mesoamerica and the central Andes fall into two broad types. One, the Synchoritic Urban type, is that found in most of the world today: a network of cities and towns, each in symbiotic relationship with its own agricultural hinterland and with other loci in the network, each a focus (to varying degrees) of multiple functions such as government, religion, manufacture, marketing, and the military. The other, the Rural Nucleated type, is less familiar to twentieth-century man. In this type of society the population is almost entirely rural, living in little villages or scattered households. The functions of church and state are carried on in "ceremonial" centers peopled only by administrators, priests, and their retainers and helpers; markets and craft centers are located in the countryside settlements. Lines of authority in this type of society may have been somewhat more diffuse, and political boundaries less exact, than in Synchoritic Urban societies.

As we shall see, these two types of society represent separate lines of sociopolitical evolution. Neither was a stage in the development of the other. Rather they were alternative—and almost equally successful—solutions to similar organizational problems. A third type, which may have been endemic in Colombia and Ecuador, appears in the archaeological records of Mesoamerica and the central Andes only as an evanescent stage in the development of Synchoritic Urbanism or as a brief fission product of its disintegration. This type is Achoritic Urbanism: a system of cities, few in number and with sparsely populated hinterlands. In this type almost everyone, even the farmer, lives in town, and each city is a more-or-less autonomous political unit, though it may federate with others for particular purposes. Achoritic Urbanism—except for the loss of political autonomy—survives in many parts of the world today.

Since the economic base of all civilizations is agriculture, with or without animal husbandry, we may begin our inquiry with the beginnings of food production far back in the Holocene. In both Peru and Mexico, cultivation was under way by or before 5000 B.C. Still earlier dates may some day be found in northwestern South

America, Central America, or perhaps the rain forests of eastern South America, but so far we do not have any preserved plant remains of appropriate antiquity from these areas. In Peru and Mexico, it seems clear that the earliest farmers were bands of hunters and gatherers living in the highlands. The first cultigens were, therefore, native plants adapted to the relatively dry climate of those highlands. They must have been fairly drought-resistant and, in some cases, frost-resistant as well.

For many millennia after the onset of cultivation, there was no great change in the demographic or societal conditions of the new farmers. They continued their nomadic, food-gathering way of life in small bands that only briefly got together in larger communities. Food crops, though acquired by somewhat different techniques, were only part of the larger, varied diet of wild foods. That the new food sources did not set off any great population explosion can be attributed to the low yield of the earliest cultigens and—at least in Peru—to periodic droughts, which would have wiped out any population gains made during good years.

When this way of life began to change, it was not in the highlands where farming had originated. The transformation began, rather, with the introduction of farming to the relatively well-watered lowlands. This transfer led quickly to rapid population growth and to the establishment of permanent, sedentary settlements. There were probably several reasons for these changes. For one thing, the lowlands had large, secure protein resources that could be acquired with favorable input-output ratios (i.e., with the expenditure of relatively little energy per unit of production) and without moving through a seasonal round. These resources, of course, were those of the shore and the ocean, whether fish and turtles from the lagoons of the Gulf coast or shellfish and sea lions from the beaches and rocky points of Peru. Since these major resources were available year-round at any given place, the addition of a minimum of cultivated plant foods to the diet eliminated the need for continuous movement in search of seasonally ripening foods. There were, in these areas, natural preconditions for sedentism.

Cereals and roots, to the extent that they were grown, increased the calorie content of an otherwise high-protein diet without, at first, seriously diminishing the input-output ratios. The human population, like that of any other animal, began to grow toward a new equilibrium with its readily available energy sources. Sedentism itself may have contributed further to the population growth, making shorter birth intervals feasible and eliminating the need for such typical nomad practices as female infanticide. Furthermore, the process may have been self-accelerative, since freedom from drought may have led to the rapid evolution of nonresistant strains (especially of cereals) with higher per acre yields, thus augmenting the calorie supply.

The effects of these processes are especially evident on the Peruvian coast, where, between 2500 B.C. and 1750 B.C., the number of farming and fishing villages multiplied rapidly until almost every good location was occupied. Though the evidence for population growth is less clear in Mesoamerica, there, too, the earliest sedentary villages (some as old as 2400 B.C.) are found in the lowlands. In both areas, also, it is the lowlands that saw the rise of the first civilizations not many centuries after the introduction of cultivation. It is at this point that the culture history of these areas diverges drastically from that of the rest of the Americas.

The earliest civilizations in Peru, as evidenced by their monumental architecture and Rural Nucleated settlement organization, were those of La Florida (c. 1750 B.C.) and Las Haldas (c. 1600 B.C.). While still older ones may some day be found, it is doubtful that they will be more than a century or two older. In Mexico we know of no civilization older than that of the Olmecs (c. 1250 B.C.), which was already so highly developed that we may expect some day to find antecedent societies hundreds of years older. The earliest periods of civilization are thus best examined on the basis of the more complete Peruvian evidence.

Several features of the earliest Peruvian civilizations are both apparent and significant: (1) They came into being before the transition from wild to cultivated foods was complete and were based on a mixed economy in which farming and herding were not necessarily the major elements. (2) To the extent that they relied on irrigation, it was only on a small, single-community scale. (3) They had populations significantly denser than those of other areas at the same time, though far below the levels that were ultimately achieved in the Early Intermediate Period. (4) They were of Rural Nucleated type. And (5) they had a geographical focus, a point of infection as it were, from which the new forms of society gradually spread out. This core area covered about 200 miles of the central and north-central coast of Peru and quickly came to include the fairly well-watered north-central highlands.

It is not easy to see why communities of farmers and fishermen should give up their autonomy to the extent of donating the enormous amounts of time and energy that went into the building of the main pyramid at La Florida. How could some one group acquire the authority to pre-empt the labor force of a dozen or more communities? This question is perhaps the key one in the understanding of the transformation to civilization, because the redistribution of power implicit in social stratification and central authority is what most distinguishes civilizations from other kinds of societies.

It is not enough to say that large, dense populations cannot be held together by older forms of organization based on kinship and locality and that therefore new forms had to evolve. What we need is a specific mechanism that controlled the evolution of specific new forms of society. Morton H. Fried has proposed that such authority was acquired when one group successfully denied to others access to basic resources—i.e., to staple foods and/or fundamental raw materials. Michael J. Harner and I have suggested independently, on the basis of quite different kinds of evidence, that such control of basic resources would be feasible specifically in cases where they were scarce due to population pressure. Where population growth has made certain basic resources scarce, and where population density is such as to provide personnel for all of the specialized statuses of a stratified, centrally organized society without detracting from the production of food, the seizure of those scarce resources by one group of people can lead very rapidly to social stratification, state organization, and civilization.

Admittedly this theory cannot now be really tested against archaeological evidence, but it does fit well with the sequence of events that took place on the Peruvian coast in the centuries before the building of the great pyramid at La Florida. The multiplication of fishing villages, and the growth of population in the valleys, were accompanied by a flourishing trade in staple foodstuffs between farm and shore. Indeed, some of the earliest major centers, such as Río Seco and Chuquitanta (*c.* 1900 B.C.), may have been established to regulate this exchange. Thus we have a situation of rapid population growth and of restricted access to basic resources that would have been an ideal seminal ground for the creation of a stratified, politically centralized society. The people of Chuquitanta and Río Seco, if indeed they controlled the flow of foodstuffs, may have provided the first ruling classes in Peru.

The tendency of civilization to spread out from its nuclear zone is readily understandable if we think of its adaptive advantages in situations of intense competition for limited resources. If there is actual fighting for territory, the little state that can mobilize the manpower of many communities has an obvious numerical advantage over any number of autonomous communities that do not act in full concert. Even where there is no direct conflict, the state has means (discussed below) of increasing food production and of more efficiently exploiting other resources, thus better accommodating its citizens. In either case, there would be powerful incentive for its neighbors to copy the new forms of organization— if, indeed, they were not already evolving them in response to the same economic/demographic conditions.

Once the first little states appear on the scene, certain broad tendencies become apparent. One of these is the continuation of population growth, accompanied by increased dependence on agriculture and animal husbandry and by a number of methods for increasing agricultural productivity. Another is interregional warfare. A third, only partly a product of such warfare, is alternation between periods characterized by small, independent regional states and periods of larger unification.

The first period of unification is represented by Chavín in Peru and Olmec in Mexico. Both were Rural Nucleated societies practicing small-scale water control (irrigation probably in Chavín, drainage definitely in Olmec), and the homeland of each lay in the core area of civilization of its respective area. Both expansions are clearly associated with religious cults, and in neither case is there clear evidence of conquest. It has been suggested that the Olmec expansion was related to the acquisition of luxury goods, especially jade; there was no similar flow of luxury goods in the Chavín domain. It has also been suggested that the Olmec cult was carried over Mesoamerica by force of arms. It is possible that both cults were spread by the sword (or, as it were, the spearthrower, sling, and war club), but there is no way of proving such a hypothesis at this time. We can say that Olmec and Chavín influences were felt far beyond their homelands, but we cannot say why with any certainty.

The Olmecs may have carried civilization into the Mexican highlands. In the Tehuacán Valley, the first water-control system (a dam) and the earliest evidence of highlands civilization appear simultaneously with the first Olmec influence, about 800 B.C. It looks very much as if the Olmecs carried their state organization into the Mexican highlands—an action that seems to imply conquest—and simultaneously introduced the water-control techniques that would free the highlanders from dependence on the uncertainties of rainfall. The Chavín expansion carried Rural Nucleated organization over all of the northern half of Peru, but there is no evidence as yet that water-control systems were associated with this spread of civilization.

Just as we cannot be sure of the reasons for the Olmec and Chavín expansions, so also we do not know why their hegemony disintegrated after a few centuries. It may have been due to the rise of other regional states capable of competing with them on equal terms. At any rate, with the waning of their influence, both Peru and Mesoamerica show a common pattern of numerous small regional states interacting in various ways. It is at this time (Late Preclassic in Mexico, Early Intermediate Period in Peru) that civilization spread nearly to its final limits, that irrigation achieved whatever importance it was ultimately to have, and that Synchoritic Urban states grew up in those areas not already organized in Rural Nucleated systems. It was also at this time—at least in Peru—that interregional warfare became endemic, and that population density reached its first maximum.

These processes are closely related to each other. The major irrigation systems of the Peruvian coast, for example, were not dug until population had grown essentially to the limits of the carrying capacity of the river valleys. The irrigation systems were a response to population pressure on resources. At the same time, they were a way of remodeling the environment to increase its productivity, and they permitted the population explosion to continue. Interregional warfare, too, can be seen as a response to population pressure, since its effect could have been (and in some cases clearly was) the acquisition of arable land to feed an over-large population. Even the growth of cities can be seen as a response to increasing population, since it is an efficient method of housing and administering large numbers of people.

Perhaps the most difficult process to understand is the divergent evolution of Rural Nucleated and Synchoritic Urban societies in Peru. In Mesoamerica each type is clearly associated with a particular environmental zone: Rural Nucleated in the wet, tropical lowlands, Synchoritic Urban in the highlands. The reasons for this difference seem clear. There are many factors in tropical forest life that lead to the dispersal of population: the prolonged fallowing of fields, the dispersal of protein resources, the scarcity of firewood in any one zone, and so on. Even when populations reach fairly dense levels, as they did in Maya country, there would be a natural tendency for people to scatter over the countryside rather than to concentrate into cities. These restrictions are not found in the highlands environments, where cities could grow up for defensive purposes, for administrative convenience, or for other reasons.

In Peru, however, the two types of states evolved in essentially the same environments, Rural Nucleated in the north and Synchoritic Urban in the south. They seem to have been alternate solutions to the problem of organizing large, dense populations. About all that one can say is that the Rural Nucleated type grew up first and that, because it evolved in the north, it had time to spread over northern Peru before cities began to grow in the south. When southern Peru evolved an urban way of life, Rural Nucleated civilization could spread no farther. At the same time, the old northern type of organization was retained until the Huari conquest put an end to it.

These regional states, with probable average populations of a few hundred thousand people, appear to me as the "normal" organizations of both Peru and Mesoamerica. They were occasionally conquered and incorporated into empires, but the latter never lasted more than a few centuries. The regional states, on the other hand, were stable entities that were repeatedly re-established whenever empires broke up.

What, then, of the famous empires? Why did Huari, Chan Chan, Cuzco, Teotihuacán, Tula, Tenochtitlán, and perhaps Tiahuanaco set out to conquer their neighbors? And why was the Aztec "empire" so different in form and organization from that of the Incas?

Empires can be recognized archaeologically in part by the widespread distribution of dominant luxury styles found at important centers and largely by the distribution of the architectural style of the conqueror. Administrative centers, garrisons, warehouses, and other buildings, all in the style characteristic of the capital, were built in the provinces to facilitate administration and guarantee pacification. By these criteria, Huari, Chan Chan, Cuzco, Teotihuacán, and probably Tula conquered large areas and organized them into superstates, whereas the Aztecs conquered but did not impose a tight organization (as we know also from the historical literature).

It is interesting that the two major Peruvian empires—those of Huari and the Incas—expanded at times of peak population density and, in each case, shortly after the onset of prolonged dry conditions in the Andes. Both of them, too, emanated from the southern highlands, an area that is subject to severe droughts even today. One may venture that the conquest of empire was a means of ensuring the food supply by incorporating large amounts of better-watered land into the state. We may note that storehouses were very prominent on the Inca landscape and that in bad times the food from them was in fact distributed to the general populace.

Yet overpopulation and drought cannot explain all empires. The Chimor empire was conquered from Chan Chan on the fertile north coast of Peru—an area that surely would not have been affected seriously by drought conditions. I can offer no explanation of the Chimor conquests, though I suspect that they again have something to do with population pressure.

For Mesoamerica it has been suggested that the Teotihuacán expansion served to guarantee control over key resources, especially the obsidian from which tools were made throughout the area.

The Aztecs present a special problem because, while they conquered widely, they did not incorporate most of the new territory into a single administration. Rather they were content to go home with their booty and to reconquer at a later time. The Aztec motto seems to have been "tribute, not taxes." It has been pointed out that the Aztecs probably did not have a standing army, without which it is of course impossible to garrison and rule conquered territory. But this failure seems to be more effect than cause—i.e., had they wanted to establish an empire, they could have raised a standing army. It has also been suggested that the basic difference between the Incas and Aztecs lay in their means of distributing goods. The Aztecs had a well-developed market system and a semi-independent class of traders, hence did not need an empire to guarantee their resource base. Under the Incas (and presumably the earlier Peruvian states), the flow of goods was tightly controlled by the state, and there were few or no markets. Access to resources could be ensured only by extending the central control to the regions from which the resources came.

To these reasons we may add the fact that the Aztecs were competing with other peoples nearly as powerful as themselves and might have had considerable difficulty in retaining their conquered territories if they had tried to. The Incas, on the other hand, had only one serious rival, and when Chimor was beaten they had a free hand to extend their government throughout the central Andes.

Why did these earth-shaking processes take place only in Peru and Mesoamerica and not in the surrounding or intervening areas? For some areas the answer seems obvious. The deserts to the south of Peru and the north of Mesoamerica not only lack water, but also have little land irrigable by ancient techniques. To the east of Peru, the Amazonian rain forest was thinly populated. Furthermore, insofar as populations there increased, they had half a continent in which to spread out, so no great density would have built up. The dense rain forests of southern Central America and the Pacific coast of Colombia could not support populations nearly so dense as those of, say, the Petén. In none of these areas did population ever reach the size or density that seems to be requisite to the evolution of civilization.

The fascinating question is why civilizations of Mesoamerican and Peruvian types did not evolve in Colombia and Ecuador. The highlands basins of northwestern South America are as extensive and fertile as those of Mesoamerica and Peru. The environments are as rich and diversified. The people were certainly in contact with the Mesoamericans and Peruvians. Where, then, are the great cities, the monumentual architecture, the remnants of empire?

Actually, I believe that civilization did develop in Ecuador and Colombia but that it was of Achoritic Urban type, which archaeologists and historians tend to overlook. Though based on less intensive agriculture and on lower population densities, it produced kingdoms with many of the characteristics of states, and these kingdoms were centered in settlements so large that they must be deemed cities. One Chibcha city near Bogotá, for example, measured two kilometers by one. What distinguishes these cities from their Mesoamerican and Peruvian counterparts is their lack of monumental architecture (attested in both the archaeological and historical records) and the fact that they were not linked into a synchoritic system with large numbers of subsidiary, food-producing settlements. I would like to offer a tentative explanation of this divergence.

We have seen that cultivation began in the highlands of Mesoamerica and Peru but that the first strides toward civilization were taken in the coastal lowlands after farming was transferred to them. These first steps were associated with, and largely dependent on, rapid population growth due to a guaranteed water supply and a natural balance of (cultivated) carbohydrates and (stable wild) proteins. In Colombia and Ecuador there are few zones with these characteristics, and these are all relatively small. The southern coast of Ecuador, for example, is a desert without the permanent rivers that characterize the Peruvian coast. The Pacific coast of Colombia is covered with impenetrable rain forest. More than half of the Caribbean coast of Colombia suffers from a prolonged dry period that leaves a growing season too short for successful farming. Cultivation in the highlands of both countries was dependent on the vagaries of rainfall. Nowhere was there a really large area with the conditions for rapid population increase that were found in Peru and Mesoamerica. Lowlands populations grew slowly or remained stable. Water control systems were not invented in the highlands, and populations there also grew slowly or remained stable.

When the peoples of northwestern South America adopted a sedentary way of life, there was no great population pressure on basic resources. Communities could and did retain their economic and political autonomy for a very long time. When populations did increase in certain regions under favorable conditions, these communities simply grew with it until they became small cities. If they divided into two or more settlements, the new towns continued to be ruled by the chief of the original city, by way of subordinate chiefs in each town. In this way small kingdoms grew up. The best known of them were those of the Chibcha in Colombia, who were thriving when the Spanish arrived. Others, such as Guangala, are known from the archaeological record. None of them seems to have had the stability of the Peruvian and Mesoamerican regional states. They thrived for a few centuries, then faded back into the pattern of small autonomous communities so characteristic of the area as a whole.

Thus conditions in northwestern South America were not so favorable for the growth of civilization as those in Mesoamerica and Peru, and the complex interactions that conditioned the evolution of civilization in the latter areas did not take place. Agriculture was less intensive and was dependent on rainfall. Population levels remained relatively low. State-like organizations grew up here and there under special circumstances, but they never took firm root.

The above is clearly not the whole story of the evolution of civilization in Mesoamerica and Peru, but I believe that it does outline the most basic processes. Many different factors interacted— environment, agriculture, highlands-lowlands interchange, resource distribution and movement, population size and density, settlement patterns, technology, and sociopolitical systems. Each of these affected the others and was affected by them; none is clearly cause or effect except at particular moments in particular processes. The whole system evolved together, changes in any one part bringing about changes in others, some of which again required readjustment of the system as a whole. Small wonder that civilizations have evolved so rarely in human history!

· BIBLIOGRAPHIC ESSAY

The literature on the evolution of civilization is enormous. In its modern form it dates back to the middle of the nineteenth century. Rather than attempting to cite it all, I believe it sufficient to mention a few of the most recent and sophisticated theses. We may begin with Julian Steward, *Theory of Culture Change* (Urbana, Ill.: University of Illinois Press, 1955), which proposes a system of multilinear evolution not overly different from that used in this chapter. Elman Service's *Primitive Social Organization: An Evolutionary Perspective* (New York: Random House, 1962), on the other hand, suggests a unilineal system of sociopolitical stages through which all of humanity has evolved or is in the process of evolving. An archaeological application of this theory, with substantial discussion of ecological and demographic factors as causes of change, is *Mesoamerica: The Evolution of a Civilization* (New York: Random House, 1968), by William Sanders and Barbara Price. Finally, Morton Fried's *The Evolution of Political Society* (New York: Random House, 1967), may be the best book ever written on the subject of the development of civilization. Though it is again praised in unilineal terms, it gives flexible and highly materialistic definitions of its stages of sociopolitical evolution and contains excellent and lengthy discussions of the causes of major changes in this realm.

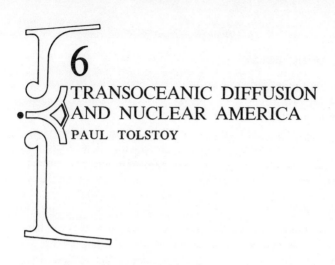

6
TRANSOCEANIC DIFFUSION
AND NUCLEAR AMERICA
PAUL TOLSTOY

· GENERAL CONSIDERATIONS

It has been customary to think of the Americas before Columbus as essentially cut off from the rest of the world. In a relative sense, this view is surely correct, as it is correct, also, of Australia or Polynesia. The mere fact, however, that it is not absolutely accurate raises the question of how numerous and how important contacts with the outside may have been at various times. Interesting in itself, this question is in turn but a prelude to gauging the importance of such contacts as stimuli and as constraints to the developing cultures of the New World.

There is considerable agreement, of course, that the peopling of the Americas took place through Bering Strait, as hunting and gathering groups moved out of Asia into North America in the Pleistocene and later lived and dispersed over both continents of the Western Hemisphere. This agreement, moreover, stems as much from the data of physical anthropology, linguistics, and ethnography as it does from those of archaeology. It is thus generally recognized that, on one occasion at least, Old World cultural events impinged significantly on those of the New.

Major uncertainties remain, however, as to whether the initial entry of man into North America was followed by others and, if so, by how many; and as to which customs and equipment may have been brought by migrants, which spread by diffusion out of Asia unaccompanied by people, and which were devised locally to meet local needs. There is finally the vexing but important question of transoceanic contacts, whereby cultural features may have been introduced into the Americas—again, it would seem, mainly from Asia—by sea-borne travelers, well after both continents had been settled.

Over the last forty years, this last question has suffered from studied neglect. As a result, there is insufficient awareness among students today of the rather large body of relevant evidence that earlier scholars have examined, debated, and accepted or rejected on the basis of a variety of arguments and criteria.

What follows is not a complete inventory of this evidence or a serious critique of any part of it. It is rather a checklist of items, a few of them new, most of them old, which deserve attention and further study if the problem is to be considered seriously at all.

· BIOLOGICAL EVIDENCE

Understandably, the presence of identical species of domesticated plants or animals in both hemispheres before 1492 has been looked upon as "hard" evidence of sea-borne contact, since genetic sameness in domesticates generally implies geologically recent dispersal from a single center. Such dispersal, moreover, is unlikely or impossible through Bering Strait and the Arctic for most of these species, for cultural as well as environmental reasons. And though the dispersal of domesticates does not always involve transport by man, it is likely to do so and, in any event, is often almost necessarily transoceanic.

It must be emphasized, therefore, that, of the dozen or so domesticates which *may* have been carried by man to or from the Americas prior to European discovery, none, except possibly the peanut, presently require travel by human groups to explain their distribution. Only three (cotton, the gourd, and the peanut) are known conclusively now to be pre-Columbian in both hemispheres.

The gourd (*Lagenaria siceraria*) was grown on the fringes of Mesoamerica *c.* 7000 B.C. (in the Ocampo phase of Tamaulipas) and in coastal Peru by 5000 B.C. (Canario phase of the Lurín Valley). It was cultivated as early as 7000 B.C. in Southeast Asia and, on botanical grounds, is thought by some to be of African origin.

Experiments show that it could have drifted across either ocean and retained its viability on arrival. However, since it is not a strand plant, "introduction by human transportation remains a distinct possibility." The case of the New World cultivated cottons (*Gossypium hirsutum* and *G. barbadense*) is somewhat different. Both are thought by some to be hybrids of a wild native cotton and a cultivated Old World species, perhaps *G. herbaceum*. Cultivated cotton is definitely pre-Columbian in the Old World, being found at Mohenjo Daro *c.* 2000 B.C., and goes back at least to 3000 B.C. in Mesoamerica and on the coast of Peru. Contact between the hemispheres is thus suggested. However, recent studies reported by J. Sauer indicate that a wild cotton found today on the coast of Yucatán, originally thought to have escaped from cultivation, may, in fact, be the sought-for native ancestor of the cultivated American cottons. The peanut (*Arachis hypogea*), an American plant known from deposits of *c.* 1800 B.C. in Peru and from the Classic Period of Mesoamerica, has recently been identified at Ch'ien Shan Yang, a Neolithic site in the Lung Shan tradition in Chekiang province, China, and at a Neolithic site in Kiangsi province, according to K. C. Chang. If confirmed, these finds could become crucial pieces of evidence for pre-Columbian travel between the hemispheres in the second millennium B.C.

Domesticates of Old World origin that may be ancient in the Americas include the coconut palm (*Cocos nucifera*), whose early presence in Central America is inferred on documentary grounds but which is capable of natural sea-borne dispersal; and the plantain (*Musa paradisiaca normalis*), of uncertain pre-Columbian status.

There is also evidence—all of it inconclusive—for the pre-Columbian travel from the New World to the Old of some American cottons (found in Polynesia and in the Cape Verde Islands off Africa in conditions suggestive of pre-European arrival); of the sweet potato; of the *jícama* (*Pachyrhyzus*); of two species of *Hibiscus;* of the grain amaranths; and of maize, the latter said to be mentioned in Chinese sources of the thirteenth and fifteenth centuries. Morris Swadesh notes that some terms for sweet potato and for *Hibiscus* in Oceania may be cognates of South American names for these plants. So far, however, the presence of these species at a suitably early date in the Old World has not been demonstrated archaeologically.

Two animals have been considered by R. Gilmore and G. Carter: the chicken, of which a rumpless, blue-egged variety may have been kept in the Andean area before Spanish arrival; and the hairless edible dog of western Mexico, which, with the practices of fattening and castration, has been proposed as an import from China. Neither of these cases is proven: the first for lack of archaeological evidence; the second, because derivation from local breeds is an obvious alternative, pending detailed studies.

Cultural features interpreted by some to indicate ancient seaborne contacts with the Old World are broadly distributed in the Americas but tend to be concentrated in two areas: northwestern South America (the northern Andean region, Central America and, often, the northern and western edges of the Amazon Basin) and Mesoamerica. Some, such as houses on piles, vine bridges or brother-sister marriage are unconvincing as evidence because they are among a limited number of possible responses to recurring needs. Others, such as cognates between Australian and Patagonian languages, the spearthrower, the sling, bull-roarers, joint amputation, and many others probably go back to Paleoamerican times and, if derived from the Old World, could have entered the Americas through Bering Strait. Such traits will be ignored in the following discussion, not because none could have come to the New World by sea, but because their weight as evidence for diffusion is negligible.

· TRAITS OF POSSIBLE EAST ASIAN ORIGIN IN SOUTH AMERICA

In South America, one of the earliest suspected sea-borne imports is the pottery of the Valdívia phase of coastal Ecuador, dated from 2700 to 2000 B.C. but perhaps beginning as early as 3200 B.C. Valdívia pottery—the first to appear on the west coast of South America and, perhaps, the first to be seen in the hemisphere—shares over three dozen elements of shape, decorative technique, and decoration design with evidently contemporary or slightly older pottery from the island of Kyushu in Japan. Some 75 percent of these attributes are found, in Kyushu, at three spatially, temporally, and culturally close sites: Izumi, Sobata, and Ataka. Almost 90 percent are represented in Valdívia A, the earliest of the phases recognized in Ecuador by Clifford Evans and his associates. Contrary to the assertions of several critics, this seems a remarkable degree of clustering in space and in time. That all of the parallels are not found precisely where they would fit ideally the diffusion hypothesis is not surprising. Such scatter is predictable in view of uncontrolled factors that affect both the sample of sites available and what is recovered from them. It is a reminder, in particular, that presently known sites are unlikely to include either the first Valdívia community in Ecuador or its parent community in Japan.

Late preceramic sites of the Peruvian coast (2500–1800 B.C.) yield the earliest known evidence of coca chewing and of the manufacture of bark cloth. The first has been compared to Southeast Asian betel chewing, which it resembles in some ways (consumption with lime of leaves containing a narcotic; associated containers, spatulas). The second—as known ethnographically from South and Central America—shares a number of unusual details of manufacturing procedure with certain bark-cloth industries of Southeast Asia that form there the Marginal group. These details include a double procedure for bark removal, on-steam beating, transversely-grooved wooden beaters, soaking after, rather than before, beating, and others. Such traits have not been and cannot be, for the most part, ascertained archaeologically, but their ethnographic distribution suggests that they form part of an industrial process from which all or many recent industries of South and Central America are derived. The scraps of bark cloth from the preceramic site of Huaca Prieta on the north coast of Peru thus provide an age estimate for this South American kind of bark cloth as a class. Again, however, there is no reason to suppose naively that Huaca Prieta is the site of its first appearance in South America or that procedures of manufacture at that site conformed precisely to the prototype reconstructed for the continent as a whole.

Cultures of somewhat later date in Ecuador exhibit features with analogies in the Far East (Machalilla, with narrow-neck bottles, carinated bowls, and line-burnishing in its ceramic inventory, probably c. 1000 B.C.; Chorrera, with earspools, c. 850–500 B.C.).

These traits, however, are among a larger number (stirrup spouts, iridescent painting, and others) that link these same cultures with Mesoamerica. If Asian derivation is to be considered for the first group of traits, the possibility must be examined that it took place not directly but by way of Mesoamerica or some yet unknown mediating center in the New World.

This alternative is also suited perhaps to the case of the Chavín style of northern Peru, in which Mesoamerican parallels (though neither abundant nor excessively strong) are combined with certain conventions that call to mind Chinese bronzes of similar date according to Robert Heine-Geldern. Chavín is also the style in which metalworking appears. Unknown to Mesoamerica at this time (?1000–500 B.C.), this craft is applied to gold in some Chavín-related cultures. Techniques include hammering, repoussé, soldering, and welding. If an Asian origin is postulated for South American metallurgy, these few techniques in northern Peru could represent an initial and still weak exposure to a trans-Pacific source or to a source already in existence elsewhere in South America.

Most of the techniques known to pre-Columbian metallurgy appear archaeologically in northern South America after Chavín times, in the course of the Early Intermediate Period. They include the smelting of copper ores (Moche), perhaps in perforated clay furnaces (*huairas*), solid and lost-wax casting (Moche), gilding (Vicús, La Tolita), granulation (Vicús, Moche), and alloying, notably of gold and copper to create *tumbaga* (Salinar). All occur in the Old World, where most of them are unquestionably pre-Columbian. However, few can be accurately dated in the Far East, where metallurgy was well developed by the end of the second millennium B.C. and may go back to the third. There is, moreover, a great scarcity of dated manufactures, both in Asia and in America, due to the reworking of metal objects in ancient times and to the more recent robbing of graves. Yet Heine-Geldern has produced a number of objects of Dong-son style from Southeast Asia (mostly bronze ornaments and cast pseudo-filigree bells of the first millennium B.C.) that share both a design and specific details (the double spiral, twisted string and braid effects, dangles) with Peruvian and Colombian jewelry. (Compare Figure 6.1.)

As evidence, metallurgy suffers from major weaknesses that stem

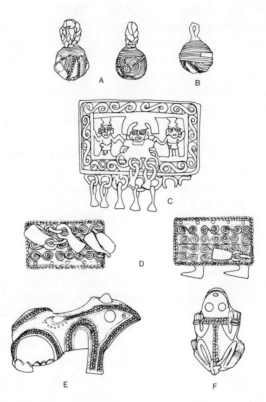

Based on photographs and illustrations in Madeleine Colani, *Les Mégalithes du Haut-Laos,* Vol. 2 (Paris: Publications de l'Ecole Française d'Extrême-Orient, 1935); G. de Créqui-Montfort and Paul Rivet, "Contribution à l'Etude de l'Archéologie et de la Métallurgie Colombiennes (avec la collaboration de H. Arsandaux, pour la partie métallurgique), *Journal de la Société des Américanistes de Paris,* n.s., t. 11 (Paris, 1914); Arthur Baessler, *Altperuanische Metallgeräte* (Berlin: Verlag von Georg Reimer, 1906); and Victor Goloubew, "L'Age du Bronze au Tonkin et dans le Nord-Annam," *Bulletin de l'Ecole Française d'Extrême-Orient,* t. 29 (Hanoi, 1930).

FIGURE 6.1   Cast metal objects from Indochina and from the Andean area of South America.   *(A)* Bronze bells, Laos.   *(B)* Bell of *tumbaga* (copper and gold alloy), Colombia.   *(C)* Silvered copper ornament, coastal Peru.   *(D)* Bronze buckles, Dong-son style, northern Viet-Nam.   *(E)* Bronze frog figure, Indochina.   *(F)* Frog figure of *tumbaga,* Colombia.

from sampling and dating problems. For this reason, even if connections with Asia are granted, it is difficult as yet to specify the phase or phases in South America initially involved or to demonstrate that all or most metallurgical parallels with the Old World first appear in America as a coherent complex in the centuries that precede and follow the beginning of our era.

In this connection, it may be important that it is in that timeband that a number of other trans-Pacific suspects appear in the Peruvian and Ecuadorian coastal sequences. Many of them figure in lists compiled by such investigators as Erland Nordenskiöld and others on the basis of ethnographic data, before their archaeological dating was possible. The more convincing include tie-dying (Paracas), the poncho-like sleeveless shirt (Paracas, Moche), panpipes (Bahía, Gallinazo, Moche, Paracas), perhaps the sailing raft (Bahía?), the neckrest (Bahía), the coolie yoke (Bahía), the blowgun (Moche), and the backstrap loom (Moche). All are ethnographically characteristic of Southeast Asia, and many have distributions in South America that extend into the Amazon Basin. Each needs further study of its formal variation and its precise distribution in Asia and in America. Together with metalworking, these traits provide some support for the idea that South American coastal settlements experienced contact with communities on the rim of the South China Sea in the centuries prior to and following the beginning of the Christian era.

Evidence favoring such distant contacts in later times is scarce in South America. One possible late introduction is the alloying of bronze, so far undemonstrated in the Americas prior to *c.* A.D. 700, when arsenic bronze appears on the coast of Peru, and tin bronze in northwestern Argentina. Attention should also be called perhaps to the paddle-stamping, press-molding, and flask shapes of late Moche and Middle Horizon pottery of northern Peru. They bring to mind the geometric style of the south China coast, and the farflung pilgrim bottles of Eurasia, whose distribution includes T'ang China. There are also the famed ceremonial clubs (*clavas insignias*), which Argentine investigators long ago compared to the similar *patu* clubs of Polynesia. This type of object could fit into the category of relatively late introductions, but its dating and context in South America still remain rather uncertain. Whether these particular introductions are granted or not, the thousand years or so preceding Spanish arrival appear relatively barren of evidence suggestive of contacts with the outside world.

· POSSIBLE SOUTHEAST ASIAN TRAITS
IN MESOAMERICA

This may not be the case so much for Mesoamerica, where parallels with Far Eastern cultures are seen by some to appear as early as 1500 B.C. and to continue as late as the Late Classic. For many of them, however, presently known dates of initial appearance are probably quite misleading in view of the sampling problems peculiar to the hieratic aspects of civilization. As Robert Rands points out, iconography, on which we are often dependent in establishing histories, all too often suggests "a vast storehouse of religious and artistic conceptions into which . . . sculptors only occasionally and sporadically dipped."

Thus, the series of 20 day-names on which the Mesoamerican calendar is based, though archaeologically attested no earlier than the Monte Albán I phase of Oaxaca, could well be older by some centuries. It shows multiple and elaborate correspondences with the Eurasian lunar zodiac and its associated deities, as identified in China, India, and the Near East by Fritz Graebner, Paul Kirchhoff, and Hugh Moran and David Kelley. This system's mere presence in Mesoamerica, in view of its arbitrary features, would seem persuasive evidence of contacts between the higher civilizations of both hemispheres. Moreover, it is but one element of an elaborately networked set of correspondences that includes mathematics (e.g., position numerals, the zero), calendrics (e.g., permutation time counts), communication devices (e.g., writing, books, paper-making), and conceptions of the world (former and present mythological worlds, world quarters and their colors, the latter with such diverse ramifications as the patolli/parchese game and state administration). To these may be added ritual practices (various forms of sacrifice, the use of water and incense, the *volador* ceremony); symbolism based on felines, snakes, and trees; and insignia of rank such as fans, parasols, and litters. With the exception of the day-names mentioned earlier and of paper-making, this vast body of evidence has yet to be approached with rigorous methods of analysis. As an undifferentiated whole, this hieratic complex may be thought to appear roughly at the time when Mesoamerica itself emerged—i.e., in the second half of the second millennium B.C. In actuality, of course, its constituent elements may have varied histories, which, as indicated earlier, it is difficult to reconstruct.

More reliably dated evidence of contacts with Asia is, predictably, less massive. On the whole, it supports the idea of multiple introductions of exotic traits over a period of time. Pottery styles appear to hold some promise in this connection. Thus, Ocós and related pre-Olmec lowland ceramics exhibit features (bottles, tripod bowls, cord-marking, zoned punctation, line burnishing, dentate stamping, shell stamping) compatible with a generic relationship with the Neolithic ceramics of Southeast Asia, even though several occur earlier in South America. These features do not survive generally into the Olmec-San Lorenzo style. However, the roughly contemporaneous grave pottery of Tlatilco in the highlands (*c.* 1000 B.C.?) retains a few (bottles, tripod bowls) and appears to add a new set (fruit-stands with openwork bases, tripod *ollas,* tetrapods, square forms) specifically reminiscent of the Lungshanoid ware of South China and Southeast Asia (Figure 6.2). A century or so later, the potstand and the carinated bowl appear (Figure 6.2); in Southeast Asia, these are favored in the Ban Kao-related ceramics of Thailand and Malaya. Then, *c.* 500 B.C., comes the teapot-like spouted vessel. Classic times see the appearance of two kinds of lidded cylindrical tripod that resemble roughly contemporary Han bronzes both in overall design and in detail, according to Gordon Ekholm. It is worth noting that these resemblances appear in an order congruent with their dating and sequence in Asia.

Contact with contemporary cultures of Southeast Asia is also suggested by the abundant occurrence in Mesoamerica of two types of bark beater, both of which date back at least to late Preclassic times in the Pacific slope region of Guatemala and El Salvador and become widespread in Classic times. They not only have precise equivalents in the Neolithic of Viet-Nam, Taiwan, the Philippines, and Celebes but, in the last region, survive into

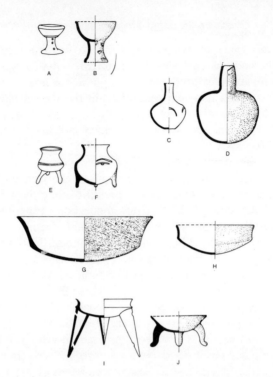

Based on illustrations in K. C. Chang, "Prehistoric Ceramic Horizons in Southeastern China and Their Extensions into Formosa," *Asian Perspectives*, Vol. 7, Nos. 1–2 (Hong Kong, 1964); Roman Piña Chán, *Tlatilco* (Córdoba, Mexico: Instituto Nacional de Antropología e Historia, 1958); W. G. Solheim II, *The Archaeology of the Central Philippines, a Study Chiefly of the Iron Age and Its Relationships* (Manila: Philippines National Institute of Science and Technology, 1964), Monograph 10; G. de G. Sieveking, "Excavations at Gua Cha, Kelantan," Parts I and II, *Federation Museums Journal*, n.s., Vols. 2–3 (Kuala Lumpur, Malaysia, 1954–55); and B. A. V. Peacock, "A Short Description of Malayan Prehistoric Pottery," *Asian Perspectives*, Vol. 3, No. 2 (Hong Kong, 1961).

FIGURE 6.2   Pottery from South China, Southeast Asia, and Mesoamerica.   *(A, B)* Pedestal cups with perforated bases: *A* from Pei-yin-yang-ying, southeast coastal plain of China, third millennium B.C.; *B* from Tlatilco, *c.* 1000 B.C.   *(C, D)* Tubular-neck bottles: *C* from Tlatilco; *D* from Kalanay site, Masbate, Philippines, late first millennium B.C. (?).   *(E, F)* Globular tripods: *E* from Pei-yin-yang-ying; *F* from Tlatilco.   *(G, H)* Carinated bowls: *G* from Gua Cha, Kelantan, Malaya, first millennium B.C. (?); *H* from Zacatenco phase, Tlatilco, 900–500 B.C.   *(I, J)* Tripod bowls: *I* from Gua Berhala, Kedah, Malaya, second millennium B.C. (?); *J* from Tlatilco.

the ethnographic present as part of a craft virtually identical to the paper-making of Mexico today and in Conquest times.

Other indications, more or less convincing, of Far Eastern contacts include: the emphasis on jade and on feline representations in Olmec culture, which recall similar orientations in the contemporary civilization of Shang China; iron-ore mirrors, flat or concave, which appear first in Olmec times and may have been inspired, perhaps repeatedly, by metal prototypes; the scroll and other motifs of the Tajín style, so similar to those on the bronzes of the Chou period; wheeled animal figures of clay, of Classic date in Mesoamerica, where the wheel was otherwise unknown (as it was altogether in the New World); and some three dozen elements of Classic Maya art and architecture that Ekholm assigns to his "Complex A," a group of traits he believes are derived from the Indo-Buddhist tradition of Southeast Asia. Complex A includes elements of architectural design and decoration (e.g., the trefoil arch, engaged colonnettes, inner sanctuaries); attributes of humans, animals, and plants shown in Maya sculpture (e.g., postures of human figures, ways of representing the water-lily); religious themes (sacred trees, the diving god, the sun disk); and attributes of status (thrones, staffs, umbrellas, fans, the litter). They tend to cluster in late Classic and early Postclassic Maya contexts, though some have earlier histories and occur elsewhere in Mesoamerica. While their dating is imprecise for reasons already stated (the quotation of Rands given above is taken from the study of water-lily representations), the time-span of their occurrences is roughly compatible with that of the domination of parts of Southeast Asia by Indian civilizations in the first millennium of our era.

· OTHER CONTACTS

Pre-Columbian ocean-borne contacts between the two worlds were quite certainly not limited to visits across the Pacific by Far Eastern voyagers, even though, in the present writer's opinion at least, the bulk of the evidence for long-range contacts does indeed suggest such visits.

Thus we know that the Norse not only settled in Greenland among the Eskimos but reached the shores of Newfoundland, where the site of L'Anse-au-Meadow has provided recently the remains of a Viking house of *c.* A.D. 1000. Earlier trans-Atlantic voyages have been argued, if not very convincingly. The botanical evidence of gourds and cotton is compatible with their introduction directly from Africa rather than Asia, according to K. H. Schwerin.

Nor, probably, should we think of the Americas as merely recipients of influence from the outside via Bering Strait or across the ocean. The possibility of the pre-Columbian spread of maize and half a dozen other domesticates to the Old World has been mentioned. Thor Heyerdahl, though he has failed to prove a substantial contribution of American elements to the culture of Polynesia, has drawn attention to certain parallels that merit further study and has shown, not only the physical possibility of westward voyages into the Pacific, but also that such voyages by Peruvians had probably taken place before Spanish arrival. Finally, there are the disturbing yet convincing linguistic and mythological correspondences long ago pointed out by David Kelley that suggest contact between Uto-Aztecan speakers and the ancestral Polynesians, near the beginning of our era, presumably in the latter's Melanesian homeland. This exciting possibility has still to receive the attention it deserves from specialists in Oceania and Mesoamerica.

· IMPLICATIONS

There is considerable disagreement over the meaning of the comparisons here reviewed. Aside from the fundamental issue of whether particular sea-borne contacts occurred or not, major topics of debate include research techniques for inferring such contacts and the importance of outside contributions to the development of native American cultures. Corollary and more concrete questions concern watercraft, routes and skills of ancient ocean voyagers, and the causes or purposes of their travels.

The last two topics are important if our vision is to progress beyond the inference of events to the inference of processes. They are also points which, in a debate that has dwelled largely on the mere existence or nonexistence of contact, have been insufficiently explored. Moreover, our knowledge of such matters as the history of watercraft on either shore of the Pacific is scant. Speculative grounds do exist for attributing sailing rafts and adequate navigational capabilities to the Neolithic inhabitants of the South China Sea area. By A.D. 400, ships sailing between Java and northern China were evidently larger than those used by Columbus. As to the causes of contacts, if these did occur, proposals have ranged from the involuntary drift hypothesis of Evans and his associates in the Valdívia case to Heine-Geldern's notion that gold prospectors from Southeast Asia introduced metallurgy in South America and that Buddhist missionaries brought "Complex A" to the Maya area. Until the facts of contact are better understood, such proposals will continue to seem highly speculative. Perhaps the soundest position as to both the mode and the motivation of early trans-Pacific travel is that nothing about them is certain enough at present to influence our judgment as to whether contacts did or did not occur. On the contrary, it is from our findings on the latter question that we may hope, in due course, to improve our understanding of the causes and concrete circumstances of these events.

Procedures appropriate for weighing the evidence for long-range diffusion cannot be discussed here. It will be enough to note that a number of tests or criteria can be advanced which, though costly of research time, should help eventually discriminate between evidence that, quantitatively and qualitatively, cannot be explained except by diffusion and evidence that is merely suggestive or congruent. These tests have been applied so far only to the bark cloth/ paper-making complex of Mesoamerica and suggest strongly that the presence of the latter in the New World cannot be accounted for fully without invoking diffusion out of Southeast Asia. Most of the material we have reviewed in this chapter has not incurred this kind of analysis and can be evaluated, at present, only on an impressionistic basis.

The impact of outside influence on New World cultures (including whatever part of it was conveyed via Bering Strait after the initial peopling) has been minimized by most American archaeologists. Imports from the outside, when acknowledged, are widely thought of as embroidery on the homespun fabric of the native pre-Columbian traditions. And it may well be true that local causes are sufficient (as they are certainly essential) to account for such milestones of cultural evolution in the Americas as the beginnings of agriculture, the transition to sedentary life, and the emergence of the state, particularly if these causes can be shown to be demographic or ecological in nature. Nevertheless, it is good to question the manner in which judgments of the causal importance of diffusion are formed and to note some of the limitations inherent in such judgments.

In purely quantitative terms, it should be recognized that for each trait or complex which retains the recognizable stamp of its alien origin, there must be many which do not, as a result, perhaps, of their essential simplicity, of transformations in transit or after arrival, or of a variety of sampling problems. That the mere practice of writing or the appreciation of jade are inadequate evidence of contact is clear. But if the possessors of these habits are shown to have acquired a sequence of day-names and the principles of paper-making from a group that also practiced writing and valued jade, the actual fact may well be that all of these features were conveyed together from one group to the other. This is a question of fact, yet one not easily answered even with the best of evidence. In consequence, our estimate, for example, of the debt of Mesoamerica to the complex societies of Southeast Asia can legitimately range from 5 to 50 percent or more of any overall listing of the characteristics of Mesoamerican civilization. The moral, of course, is that such estimates are best not made at all. A corollary, however, is that no sound structure can rest on the premise that trans-Pacific contributions to native American culture are numerically negligible, once we admit that such contributions took place at all.

Qualitatively, the importance of diffused material is often belittled on the grounds that culture is an adaptive mechanism, that its function is to solve certain problems, and that these problems have a limited number of solutions. Therefore, it is argued, had paper-making or the blow-gun not been introduced from the outside, local equivalents would have been devised to fill the same needs. In fact, the reasoning goes, these substitutes might so resemble the diffused item in essential ways that the distinction between the two would become trivial, as would the historical problem of distinguishing between them. This is facile and irresponsible speculation. It begs the questions, in any given case, of the precise extent to which form is determined by function and whether the need for a particular item, at a certain time and place, was ever so urgent and so specific as to cause it to appear spontaneously at the time and in the form in which we find it. These questions cannot be answered *a priori* or through hindsight. In most cases, they cannot be answered at all, regardless of whether diffusion as an event is actually indicated by the evidence.

Finally, it has been asserted that the more important "structural" or "core" features of societies and cultures (e.g., sedentary life, cities, social classes, the state) are refractory to diffusion to a degree that more trivial materials (tools, techniques, myths) are not. This is doubtless true, particularly when labels such as "cities" or "the state" are divested of specific content and defined in minimal and abstract fashion. They designate, then, some of the very few alternative solutions to the recurrent problems faced by all human societies. The definition of such abstract notions as the state, however, is but a first step in what should be a major preoccupation of the student of human cultures: at what point on the continuum from the abstract to the concrete (e.g., from "the state" to the specific forms of administration practiced by the Aztecs or the Incas) do we leave the realm of essential "structure" and enter the specific, the trivial, the easily diffused and easily borrowed? Where on this continuum do we place such features as divine kingship, a fourfold division of the realm, or particular forms of court etiquette? And if we acknowledge that some of the latter *can* be diffused and borrowed, what reasons are there to suppose that the more abstract systems of which they are part would have existed without them?

It should also be remembered that not all nonstructural, concrete, easily diffused traits are trivial in their overall effect on culture change. Maize cultivation, metallurgy, and writing are highly concrete, transmissible items that have, on occasion, been essential agents in the structural transformation of societies that adopted them. This suggests that, as in chemical compounds, structure in human societies may be generated by the bonds that its constituent elements are capable of forming among themselves.

Conversely, abstract, structural principles of sociocultural organization are not altogether immune to transmission and borrowing from society to society. Such institutional traits as centralized authority or militarism may thus be adopted by particular societies as responses to others already endowed with these features, these other societies providing both the problem and its solution to the recipients. A process of this kind is thought by Sanders and Price to have taken place upon contact between Teotihuacán and the Lowland Mayas in Classic times. It must be recognized as a form of diffusion, and one involving cultural material often thought to be difficult to transmit from one society to another.

To conclude, it is difficult at present to measure the debt of the New World cultures to those of the Old, whether in terms of amount of cultural material transmitted from one hemisphere to the other or of the importance of this material in determining the overall configuration of native pre-Columbian cultures in America. The chances are high, however, that this debt has been underestimated by most archaeologists working in the New World.

· BIBLIOGRAPHIC ESSAY

Pre-Columbian trans-Pacific contacts are the subject of a vast literature. Much of the botanical evidence for South America is mentioned, *passim*, by Carl O. Sauer in his contribution, "Cultivated Plants of South and Central America," to Vol. 6 of Julian H. Steward, ed., *Handbook of South American Indians*, Smithsonian Institution, Bureau of American Ethnology, Bulletin 143 (1950). Cotton, the gourd, the coconut, the sweet potato, and maize have been the subject of recent summary papers by, respectively, S. G. Stephens, Thomas W. Whitaker, Jonathan D. Sauer, Donald D. Brand, and M. D. W. Jeffreys, in *Man Across the Sea*, edited by Carroll L. Riley *et al.* (Austin and London: University of Texas Press, 1971). Trans-Atlantic dispersal of gourds and cotton is considered by Karl H. Schwerin in *Winds Across the Atlantic*, Research Records of the University Museum, Southern Illinois University, Carbondale (1970). Jonathan D. Sauer sees a wild indigenous variety as the possible ancestor of the American domesticated cottons in his *Geographic Reconnaissance of Seashore Vegetation Along the Mexican Gulf Coast*, Technical Report No. 56, Coastal Studies Institute, Louisiana State University, Baton Rouge (1967). The same author examines the amaranths in "The Grain Amaranths and Their Relatives," *Annals of the Missouri Botanical Garden,* Vol. 54 (1967), pp. 103–37. Archaeological evidence for the peanut in China is cited by William Watson in "Early Cereal Cultivation in China," in Peter J. Ucko and G. W. Dimbleby, eds., *The Domestication and Exploitation of Plants and Animals* (Chicago: Aldine, 1969), p. 400. George F. Carter, in a note in *American Antiquity,* Vol. 20, No. 2 (1954), pp. 176–77, has drawn attention to the work of L. van der Pijl, who suggested in 1937 that *Hibiscus* in Southeast Asia may have been a pre-Columbian import in view of its reproductive mechanism, adapted to pollination by New World humming birds. This may be significant in view of the fact that terms for that plant in South and Central America may be cognates of Austronesian terms (see O. F. Cook and R. C. Cook, "The Maho or Mahagua as a Trans-Pacific Plant," *Journal of the Washington Academy of Sciences,* Vol. 8, 1918, pp. 153–70). Work in progress by Paul Tolstoy has shown that bark cloth was manufactured from hibiscus in Southeast Asia, Oceania, and the New World, in some cases using highly similar techniques. Possible evidence for pre-Columbian chicken in America is noted by Raymond W. Gilmore, in the chapter on "Fauna and Ethnozoology of South America," Vol. 6, *Handbook of South American Indians, op. cit.,* pp. 343–463.

The case for the Japanese origin of Valdívia pottery is presented in lavish pictorial detail by Betty J. Meggers, Clifford Evans, and Emilio Estrada in *Early Formative Period of Coastal Ecuador,* Smithsonian Contributions to Anthropology, Vol. 1 (1965), and, in a shorter and more popular form, by the first two of these authors in an article in *Scientific American,* Vol. 214, No. 1 (1969), pp. 28–35, titled "A Transpacific Contact in 3000 B.C." Despite formal flaws in the presentation of the evidence, and the strictures of Donald Lathrap (*American Anthropologist,* Vol. 69, No. 1, pp. 96–98) and of Jon D. Muller (*American Antiquity,* Vol. 33, No. 2, pp. 254–55), this material appears, on balance, to be supportive of the trans-Pacific diffusion hypothesis.

The data on bark cloth industries of South America have not yet been brought together in print, but the characteristics of the Southeast Asian industries concerned in parallels with South America appear in tabular form in the "Marginal" group, in the 1963 paper by Tolstoy

referenced below in connection with Old World parallels in Meso-
america. The metallurgies of the Old and New Worlds were compared
by Robert Heine-Geldern in 1954, in an article in *Paideuma,* Vol. 5,
No. 7/8, pp. 347–423 ("Die asiatische Herkunft der süd-amerikani-
schen Metalltechnik") and, more recently, in a paper in English,
"American Metallurgy and the Old World," in N. Bernard, ed., *Early
Chinese Art and Its Possible Influence in the Pacific Basin* (New York:
Intercultural Arts Press, 1972). Ethnographic parallels between South
American and East Asian cultures have been assembled by Erland
Nordenskiöld, *Origin of the Indian Civilizations in South America,*
Comparative Ethnographic Studies, No. 9 (1931), pp. 17–19. Carroll
L. Riley has dealt with the blowgun in "The Blowgun in the New
World," *Southwestern Journal of Anthropology,* Vol. 8, No. 3 (1952),
pp. 297–319, but has avoided the specifics of transoceanic parallels.
The archaeological appearance of several suggestive traits in coastal
Ecuador is discussed by Emilio Estrada and Betty J. Meggers in "A
Complex of Traits of Probable Transpacific Origin on the Coast of
Ecuador," *American Anthropologist,* Vol. 63 (1961), pp. 913–39.
Pilgrim bottles in Eurasia are briefly noted by William Willetts in Vol. 2
of *Chinese Art,* Pelican Books, A359 (Harmondsworth, Middlesex,
1958), pp. 472–73. The "ceremonial club" problem has been summarized by Oswaldo Menghin in "Relaciones Transpacíficas de la Cultura Araucana," pp. 90–98 of *Jornadas Internacionales de Arqueología
y Etnografía,* Vol. 2 (Buenos Aires, 1962).

    The quotation of Robert L. Rands is taken from *The Water Lily in
Maya Art: A Complex of Alleged Asiatic Origin,* Smithsonian Institution, Bureau of American Ethnology, Bulletin 151 (1953). Comparisons
between the Eurasian lunar zodiac and the Mesoamerican day-names
have been made by Fritz Graebner, Paul Kirchhoff, and, most
recently and convincingly, by David H. Kelley ("Calendar Animals
and Deities," *Southwestern Journal of Anthropology,* Vol. 16, No. 3,
1960, pp. 317–37). Kelley, with Hugh A. Moran, has also written *The
Alphabet and the Ancient Calendar Signs* (Palo Alto, Calif.: Daily
Press, 1969); see Ch. 8, "American Parallels." Mesoamerica paper-
making is compared to Indonesian bark-cloth manufacture by Paul
Tolstoy in "Cultural Parallels Between Southeast Asia and Mesoamerica
in the Manufacture of Bark Cloth," *Transactions of the New York
Academy of Sciences,* Ser. II, Vol. 25, No. 6 (1963), pp. 646–62; and

"Method in Long Range Comparison," *Actas del 36 Congreso de Americanistas* (Madrid, 1966), pp. 69–89. A check-list of Old World features appearing in Mesoamerican civilization has been compiled by John L. Sorenson in "The Significance of an Apparent Relationship Between the Ancient Near East and Mesoamerica," in *Man Across the Sea,* cited earlier. Though referenced for the Near East, most of these traits occur in the other foci of civilization in Eurasia. An analysis of the patolli-parchese game was initiated by Charles J. Erasmus in "Patolli, Pachisi and the Limitation of Possibilities," *Southwestern Journal of Anthropology,* Vol. 6 (1950), pp. 369–87, but did not proceed beyond generalities.

No systematic attempt has been made yet to compare the development of ceramics in Southeast Asia and Mesoamerica, though some pottery forms common to the two areas are described by Robert Heine-Geldern in "Chinese Influence in the Pottery of Mexico, Central America, and Colombia," *Actas del 33 Congreso de Americanistas* (San José, Costa Rica, 1959), and by Gordon F. Ekholm in "Transpacific Contacts," in *Prehistoric Man in the New World,* edited by Jesse D. Jennings and Edward Norbeck (Chicago: University of Chicago Press, 1964). Ekholm also surveys a number of other archaeological parallels. "Complex A" is the subject of an earlier paper by the same author (*A Possible Focus of Asiatic Influence in the Late Classic,* Memoir 9 of *Asia and North America: Transpacific Contacts,* edited by Marion W. Smith, Society for American Archaeology, 1953, pp. 72–97).

Norse settlement in Newfoundland is reported by H. Ingstad in "Vinland Ruins Prove Vikings Found the New World," *National Geographic,* Vol. 126, No. 5 (1964). A case for a European origin of Laurentian and Woodland forms has been made by Alice B. Kehoe, "Small Boats upon the North Atlantic," in *Man Across the Sea.* Thor Heyerdahl's thesis that Polynesia was peopled from American shores is presented massively in *American Indians in the Pacific* (London: Allen and Unwin, 1952), but is weak methodologically. David H. Kelley's linguistic comparisons between Uto-Aztecan and proto-Polynesian are briefly presented in "Linguistics and Problems of Trans-Pacific Contacts," *Actas del 35 Congreso Internacional de Americanistas* (Mexico, 1964), pp. 17–19.

Recent general discussions of the trans-Pacific diffusion problem include Alfonso Caso's "Relations Between the Old and New Worlds: A Note on Methodology," *Actas del 35 Congreso Internacional de Americanistas* (Mexico, 1964), pp. 55–71; Gordon F. Ekholm's article in *Prehistoric Man in the New World,* cited earlier; Douglas Fraser's "Theoretical Issues in the Transpacific Diffusion Controversy," *Social Research,* Vol. 32, No. 4 (1965), pp. 452–77; David H. Kelley's "Diffusion: Evidence and Process," in *Man Across the Sea;* Oswaldo Menghin's "Relaciones Transpacíficas de América Precolombina," *Runa,* Vol. 10, Parts 1–2 (1967), pp. 83–97; Philip Phillips' "The Role of Transpacific Contacts in the Development of New World Pre-Columbian Civilizations," in Robert Wauchope, ed., *Handbook of Middle American Indians,* Vol. 4 (Austin: University of Texas Press, 1966), pp. 296–315; Robert Heine-Geldern's "The Problem of Transpacific Influences in Mesoamerica," *Handbook of Middle American Indians,* Vol. 4, pp. 277–95; and John H. Rowe's "Diffusionism and Archaeology," *American Antiquity,* Vol. 31, No. 3 (1966), pp. 334–37. See also rejoinder to the last by Stephen Jett and George F. Carter in *American Antiquity,* Vol. 31, No. 6 (1966), pp. 867–70; and Paul Tolstoy, "Method in Long Range Comparison," cited earlier, and "Diffusion: As Explanation and as Event," in N. Bernard, ed., *Early Chinese Art and Its Possible Influence in the Pacific Basin* (New York: Intercultural Arts Press, 1972). In the same collection, Clinton R. Edwards discusses navigation and the balsa raft, in "New World Perspectives on Pre-European Voyaging in the Pacific."

COMPLETE BIBLIOGRAPHY

Adams, R. McC., 1966, *The Evolution of Urban Society,* Aldine, Chicago.

Aveleyra Arroyo de Anda, L., 1965, "The Pleistocene Carved Bones from Tequixquiac, Mexico: A Reappraisal," *American Antiquity,* Vol. 30, No. 3, pp. 261–77.

Bell, R. E., 1958, *Guide to the Identification of Certain American Indian Projectile Points,* Oklahoma Anthropological Society, Special Bulletin 1, Oklahoma City.

————, 1960, *Guide to the Identification of Certain American Indian Projectile Points,* Oklahoma Anthropological Society, Special Bulletin 2, Oklahoma City.

Bennett, W., and J. Bird, 1949, *Andean Culture History,* American Museum of Natural History, Handbook Series, No. 15, New York.

Benson, E. P., editor, 1968, *Dumbarton Oaks Conference on the Olmec,* Dumbarton Oaks Research Library and Collection, Washington, D.C.

Bernal, I., 1963, *Mexico Before Cortez,* Dolphin Books, Doubleday, New York.

Bird, J., 1946, "The Archaeology of Patagonia," *Handbook of South American Indians,* Vol. 1, Smithsonian Institution, Bureau of American Ethnology, Bulletin 143.

146   PREHISPANIC AMERICA

————, 1969, *A Comparison of South Chilean and Ecuadorian "Fishtail" Projectile Points,* Kroeber Anthropological Society, University of California at Berkeley, Paper 40.

Bischof, H., and J. Viteri, 1972, "Pre-Valdívia Occupations on the Southwest Coast of Ecuador," *American Antiquity,* Vol. 37, No. 4, pp. 548–51.

Brand, D. D., 1971, "The Sweet Potato: An Exercise in Methodology," *Man Across the Sea: Problems of Pre-Columbian Contacts,* C. L. Riley, J. C. Kelley, C. W. Pennington, R. L. Rands, editors, University of Texas Press, Austin.

Brush, C. F., 1965, "Pox Pottery: Earliest Identified Mexican Ceramic," *Science,* Vol. 149, No. 3680, pp. 194–95.

Bryan, A. L., 1965, *Paleo-American Prehistory,* Occasional Papers of the Idaho State University Museum, No. 16, Pocatello.

Bushnell, G. H. S., 1956, *Peru,* Ancient Peoples and Places Series, Thames and Hudson, London.

Byers, D. S., editor, 1967–68, *The Prehistory of the Tehuacán Valley,* Vols. 1 and 2, University of Texas Press, Austin.

Carter, G. F., 1954, " 'Disharmony Between Asiatic Flower-birds and American Bird-flowers,' " *American Antiquity,* Vol. 20, No. 2, pp. 176–77.

————, 1971, "Pre-Columbian Chickens in America," *Man Across the Sea: Problems of Pre-Columbian Contacts,* C. L. Riley, J. C. Kelley, C. W. Pennington, R. L. Rands, editors, University of Texas Press, Austin.

Caso, A., 1964, "Relations Between the Old and New Worlds: A Note on Methodology," *Actas del 35 Congreso Internacional de Americanistas,* Vol. 1, pp. 55–71, Mexico.

Chang, K. C., 1971, *The Archaeology of Ancient China,* Yale University Press, New Haven.

Coe, M. D., 1962, *Mexico,* Ancient Peoples and Places Series, Praeger, New York.

————, 1966, *The Maya,* Praeger, New York.

————, 1968, *America's First Civilization,* American Heritage Publishing Co., New York.

Coe, M. D., and K. V. Flannery, 1966, "Microenvironments and Mesoamerican Prehistory," *Ancient Mesoamerica, Selected Readings,* J. A. Graham, editor, Peek Publications, Palo Alto, Calif.

Cook, O. F., and R. C. Cook, 1918, "The Maho or Mahagua as a Trans-Pacific Plant," *Journal of the Washington Academy of Sciences,* Vol. 8, pp. 153–70.

Covarrubias, M., 1957, *Indian Art of Mexico and Central America,* Knopf, New York.

Doran, E., Jr., 1971, "The Sailing Raft as a Great Tradition," *Man Across the Sea: Problems of Pre-Columbian Contacts,* C. L. Riley, J. C. Kelley, C. W. Pennington, R. L. Rands, editors, University of Texas Press, Austin.

Edwards, C. R., 1972, "New World Perspectives on Pre-European Voyaging in the Pacific," *Early Chinese Art and Its Possible Influence in the Pacific Basin,* N. Bernard, editor, Intercultural Arts Press, New York.

Ekholm, G. F., 1953, "A Possible Focus of Asiatic Influence in the Late Classic," *Asia and North America: Transpacific Contacts,* M. W. Smith, editor, Society for American Archaeology, Memoir 9, Washington, D.C.

———, 1964, "The Possible Chinese Origin of Teotihuacán Cylindrical Tripod Pottery and Certain Related Traits," *Actas del 35 Congreso Internacional de Americanistas,* Vol. 1, pp. 39–45, Mexico.

———, 1964, "Transpacific Contacts," *Prehistoric Man in the New World,* J. D. Jennings and E. Norbeck, editors, University of Chicago Press, Chicago.

Erasmus, C. J., 1950, "Patolli, Pachisi and the Limitation of Possibilities," *Southwestern Journal of Anthropology,* Vol. 6, No. 4, pp. 369–87.

Estrada, E., and B. J. Meggers, 1961, "A Complex of Traits of Probable Transpacific Origin on the Coast of Ecuador," *American Anthropologist,* Vol. 63, No. 5, pp. 913–39.

Evans, C., and B. J. Meggers, 1960, *Archeological Investigations in British Guiana,* Smithsonian Institution, Bureau of American Ethnology, Bulletin 177.

———, 1968, *Archeological Investigations on the Río Napo, Eastern Ecuador,* Smithsonian Contributions to Anthropology, Vol. 6.

Flannery, K. V., 1968, "Archeological Systems Theory and Early Mesoamerica," *Anthropological Archeology in the Americas,* B. J. Meggers, editor, Anthropological Society of Washington, Washington, D.C.

Fraser, D., 1965, "Theoretical Issues in the Transpacific Diffusion Controversy," *Social Research,* Vol. 32, No. 4, pp. 452–77.

Fried, M. H., 1967, *The Evolution of Political Society,* Random House, New York.

Gilmore, R. W., 1950, "Fauna and Ethnozoology of South America," *Handbook of South American Indians,* Vol. 6, Smithsonian Institution, Bureau of American Ethnology, Bulletin 143.

Graebner, F., 1921, "Alt-und neuweltliche Kalender," *Zeitschrift für Ethnologie,* Vol. 52, pp. 6–37.

Graham, J. A., editor, 1966, *Ancient Mesoamerica, Selected Readings,* Peek Publications, Palo Alto, Calif.

Green, D. F., and G. W. Lowe, 1967, *Altamira and Padre Piedra, Early Preclassic Sites in Chiapas, Mexico,* Papers of the New World Archaeological Foundation, No. 20, Provo, Utah.

Heine-Geldern, R., 1954, "Die asiatische Herkunft der süd-amerikanischen Metalltechnik," *Paideuma,* Vol. 5, Nos. 7/8, pp. 347–423.

———, 1959, "Chinese Influence in the Pottery of Mexico, Central America, and Colombia," *Actas del 33 Congreso de Americanistas,* Vol. 1, pp. 207–10, San José, Costa Rica.

Heine-Geldern, R., and G. F. Ekholm, 1951, "Significant Parallels in the Symbolic Arts of Southern Asia and Middle America," *The Civilizations of Ancient America,* Sol Tax, editor, International Congress of Americanists, Selected Papers, pp. 299–309, University of Chicago Press, Chicago.

———, 1966, "The Problem of Transpacific Influences in Mesoamerica," *Handbook of Middle American Indians,* R. Wauchope, editor, Vol. 4, University of Texas Press, Austin.

———, 1972, "American Metallurgy and the Old World," *Early Chinese Art and Its Possible Influence in the Pacific Basin,* N. Bernard, editor, Intercultural Arts Press, New York.

Heyerdahl, T., 1952, *American Indians in the Pacific,* Allen and Unwin, London.

Ingstad, H., 1964, "Vinland Ruins Prove Vikings Found the New World," *National Geographic Magazine,* Vol. 126, No. 5, pp. 708–30.

Jeffreys, M. D. W., 1967, "Who Introduced Maize into Southern Africa?" *South African Journal of Science,* Vol. 63, pp. 23–40.

————, 1971, "Pre-Columbian Maize in Asia," *Man Across the Sea: Problems of Pre-Columbian Contacts*, C. L. Riley, J. C. Kelley, C. W. Pennington, R. L. Rands, editors, University of Texas Press, Austin.

Jett, S., and G. F. Carter, 1966, "A Comment on Rowe's 'Diffusionism and Archaeology,' " *American Antiquity*, Vol. 31, No. 6, pp. 867–70.

Kehoe, A. B., 1971, "Small Boats upon the North Atlantic," *Man Across the Sea: Problems of Pre-Columbian Contacts*, C. L. Riley, J. C. Kelley, C. W. Pennington, R. L. Rands, editors, University of Texas Press, Austin.

Kelley, D. H., 1957, "Our Elder Brother Coyote," unpublished Ph.D. dissertation, Harvard University.

————, 1960, "Calendar Animals and Deities," *Southwestern Journal of Anthropology*, Vol. 16, No. 3, pp. 317–37.

————, 1964, "Knife-wing and Other Man-eating Birds," *Actas del 35 Congreso Internacional de Americanistas*, Vol. 1, pp. 589–90, Mexico.

————, 1964, "Linguistics and Problems of Trans-Pacific Contacts," *Actas del 35 Congreso Internacional de Americanistas*, Vol. 1, pp. 17–19, Mexico.

————, 1971, "Diffusion: Evidence and Process," *Man Across the Sea: Problems of Pre-Columbian Contacts*, C. L. Riley, J. C. Kelley, C. W. Pennington, R. L. Rands, editors, University of Texas Press, Austin.

Kirchhoff, P., 1964, "The Diffusion of a Great Religious System from India to Mexico," *Actas del 35 Congreso Internacional de Americanistas*, Vol. 1, pp. 73–100, Mexico.

————, 1966, "Mesoamerica," *Ancient Mesoamerica, Selected Readings*, J. A. Graham, editor, Peek Publications, Palo Alto, Calif.

Krieger, A. D., 1964, "Early Man in the New World," *Prehistoric Man in the New World*, J. D. Jennings and E. Norbeck, editors, University of Chicago Press, Chicago.

Lanning, E., 1967, *Peru Before the Incas*, Prentice-Hall, Englewood Cliffs, N.J.

————, 1970, "Pleistocene Man in South America," *World Archaeology*, Vol. 2, No. 1, pp. 90–111.

Lathrap, D., 1967, "Review of *Early Formative Period of Coastal*

Ecuador: The Valdívia and Machalilla Phases," American Anthropologist, Vol. 69, No. 1, pp. 96–98.

———, 1970, *The Upper Amazon,* Ancient Peoples and Places Series, Praeger, New York.

Lynch, T. F., 1967, *The Nature of the Central Andean Preceramic,* Occasional Papers of the Idaho State University Museum, No. 21, Pocatello.

MacNeish, R. S., 1967, "Mesoamerican Archaeology," *Biennial Review of Anthropology,* 1967, B. J. Siegel and A. R. Beals, editors, Stanford University Press, Stanford.

MacNeish, R. S., F. Peterson, and K. V. Flannery, 1970, "The Purrón Phase," *The Prehistory of the Tehuacán Valley,* Vol. 3, R. S. MacNeish, editor, University of Texas Press, Austin.

Mason, J. A., 1957, *The Ancient Civilizations of Peru,* Pelican Books, A395, Harmondsworth, Middlesex.

Meggers, B. J., 1966, *Ecuador,* Ancient Peoples and Places Series, Praeger, New York.

Meggers, B. J., and C. Evans, 1957, *Archeological Investigations at the Mouth of the Amazon,* Smithsonian Institution, Bureau of American Ethnology, Bulletin 167.

———, 1969, "A Transpacific Contact in 3000 B.C.," *Scientific American,* Vol. 214, No. 1, pp. 28–35.

Meggers, B. J., C. Evans, and E. Estrada, 1965, *Early Formative Period of Coastal Ecuador: The Valdívia and Machalilla Phases,* Smithsonian Contributions to Anthropology, Vol. 1.

Menghin, O. F. A., 1962, "Relaciones Transpacíficas de la Cultura Araucana," *Jornadas Internacionales de Arqueología y Etnografía,* Vol. 2, pp. 90–98.

———, 1967, "Relaciones Transpacíficas de América Precolombina," *Runa,* Vol. 10, Parts 1–2, pp. 83–97.

Millon, R., 1970, "Teotihuacán: Completion of Map of Giant Ancient City in the Valley of Mexico," *Science,* Vol. 170, No. 3962, pp. 1077–82.

Moran, H. A., and D. H. Kelley, 1969, *The Alphabet and the Ancient Calendar Signs,* Daily Press, Palo Alto, Calif.

Muller, J. D., 1968, "A Comment on Ford's Review of *Early Formative Period of Coastal Ecuador,*" *American Antiquity,* Vol. 33, No. 2, pp. 254–55.

Nordenskiöld, E., 1931, *Origin of the Indian Civilizations in South*

America, Comparative Ethnographical Studies, No. 9, pp. 1–153.

Patterson, B., and R. Pascual, 1968, "The Fossil Mammal Fauna of South America," *The Quarterly Review of Biology,* Vol. 43, pp. 409–51.

Pettipas, L., n.d., "New World Prehistory," manuscript in the Department of Anthropology, University of Manitoba, Winnipeg.

Phillips, P., 1966, "The Role of Transpacific Contacts in the Development of New World Pre-Columbian Civilizations," *Handbook of Middle American Indians,* R. Wauchope, editor, Vol. 4, University of Texas Press, Austin.

Prest, V. K., 1969, "Retreat of Wisconsin and Recent Ice in North America," Geological Survey of Canada, Map 1257A.

Rands, R. L., 1953, *The Water Lily in Maya Art: A Complex of Alleged Asiatic Origin,* Anthropological Papers, No. 34, Smithsonian Institution, Bureau of American Ethnology, Bulletin 151.

Reichel-Dolmatoff, G., 1965, *Colombia,* Ancient Peoples and Places Series, Praeger, New York.

Riley, C. L., 1952, "The Blowgun in the New World," *Southwestern Journal of Anthropology,* Vol. 8, No. 3, pp. 297–319.

Riley, C. L., J. C. Kelley, C. W. Pennington, and R. L. Rands, editors, 1971, *Man Across the Sea: Problems of Pre-Columbian Contacts,* University of Texas Press, Austin.

Rouse, I., and J. M. Cruxent, 1963, *Venezuelan Archaeology,* Yale University Caribbean Series, No. 6, New Haven.

Rowe, J. H., 1946, "Inca Culture at the Time of the Spanish Conquest," *Handbook of South American Indians,* Vol. 2, Smithsonian Institution, Bureau of American Ethnology, Bulletin 143.

———, 1966, "Diffusionism and Archaeology," *American Antiquity,* Vol. 31, No. 3, pp. 334–37.

Sanders, W. T., and B. J. Price, 1968, *Mesoamerica: The Evolution of a Civilization,* Random House Studies in Anthropology, AS 9, New York.

Sauer, C. O., 1950, "Cultivated Plants of South and Central America," *Handbook of South American Indians,* Vol. 6, Smithsonian Institution, Bureau of American Ethnology, Bulletin 143.

Sauer, J. D., 1967, *Geographic Reconnaissance of Seashore Vegetation Along the Mexican Gulf Coast,* Coastal Studies Institute, Louisiana State University, Technical Report No. 56, Baton Rouge.

———, 1967, "The Grain Amaranths and Their Relatives: A Revised

Taxonomic and Geographic Survey," *Annals of the Missouri Botanical Gardens,* Vol. 54, No. 2, pp. 103–37.

Sauer, J. D., 1971, "A Reevaluation of the Coconut as an Indicator of Human Dispersal," *Man Across the Sea: Problems of Pre-Columbian Contacts,* C. L. Riley, J. C. Kelley, C. W. Pennington, R. L. Rands, editors, University of Texas Press, Austin.

Schwerin, K. H., 1970, *Winds Across the Atlantic: Possible African Origins for Some Pre-Columbian New World Cultures,* Mesoamerican Studies, Research Records, University Museum of Southern Illinois University, No. 6, Carbondale.

Service, E., 1962, *Primitive Social Organization: An Evolutionary Perspective,* Random House, New York.

Sociedad Mexicana de Antropología, 1966, *Teotihuacán,* Onceava Mesa Redonda, Mexico.

Solheim, W. G., 1967, "Southeast Asia and the West," *Science,* Vol. 157, No. 3791, pp. 896–902.

Sorenson, J. L., 1971, "The Significance of an Apparent Relationship Between the Ancient Near East and Mesoamerica," *Man Across the Sea: Problems of Pre-Columbian Contacts,* C. L. Riley, J. C. Kelley, C. W. Pennington, R. L. Rands, editors, University of Texas Press, Austin.

Stephens, S. G., 1971, "Some Problems of Interpreting Transoceanic Dispersal of the New World Cottons," *Man Across the Sea: Problems of Pre-Columbian Contacts,* C. L. Riley, J. C. Kelley, C. W. Pennington, R. L. Rands, editors, University of Texas Press, Austin.

Steward, J., 1955, *Theory of Culture Change,* University of Illinois Press, Urbana.

Swadesh, M., 1964, "Linguistic Overview," *Prehistoric Man in the New World,* J. D. Jennings and E. Norbeck, editors, University of Chicago Press, Chicago.

Thompson, J. E. S., 1966, *The Rise and Fall of Maya Civilization,* University of Oklahoma Press, Norman.

Tolstoy, P., 1963, "Cultural Parallels Between Southeast Asia and Mesoamerica in the Manufacture of Bark Cloth," *Transactions of the New York Academy of Sciences,* Ser. II, Vol. 25, No. 6, pp. 646–62.

———, 1966, "Method in Long Range Comparison," *Actas del 36 Congreso de Americanistas,* Vol. 1, pp. 69–89, Madrid.

————, 1969, "Review of *Mesoamerica: The Evolution of a Civilization* by William T. Sanders and B. Price," *American Anthropologist,* Vol. 71, No. 3, pp. 554–58.

————, 1972, "Diffusion: As Explanation and as Event," *Early Chinese Art and Its Possible Influence in the Pacific Basin,* N. Bernard, editor, Intercultural Arts Press, New York.

Tolstoy, P., and L. Paradis, 1970, "Early and Middle Preclassic Culture in the Basin of Mexico," *Science,* Vol. 167, No. 3917, pp. 344–51.

Vaillant, G. C., 1950, *Aztecs of Mexico,* Pelican Books, A200, Harmondsworth, Middlesex.

van der Pijl, L., 1937, "Disharmony Between Asiatic Flower-birds and American Bird-flowers," *Annales du Jardin Botanique de Buitenzorg,* Vol. 48, Part 1, pp. 17–26.

Watson, W., 1969, "Early Cereal Cultivation in China," *The Domestication and Exploitation of Plants and Animals,* P. J. Ucko and G. W. Dimbleby, editors, Aldine, Chicago.

Wauchope, R., editor, 1965–66, *Handbook of Middle American Indians,* Volumes 2, 3, and 4, University of Texas Press, Austin.

Whitaker, T. W., 1971, "Endemidon and Pre-Columbian Migration of the Bottle Gourd, *Lagenaria licerariz* (Mol.) Standl.," *Man Across the Sea: Problems of Pre-Columbian Contacts,* C. L. Riley, J. C. Kelley, C. W. Pennington, R. L. Rands, editors, University of Texas Press, Austin.

Willets, W., 1958, *Chinese Art,* 2 vols., Pelican Books, A359, Harmondsworth, Middlesex.

Willey, G., 1953, *Prehistoric Settlement Patterns in the Virú Valley,* Smithsonian Institution, Bureau of American Ethnology, Bulletin 155.

Wolf, E., 1962, *Sons of the Shaking Earth,* University of Chicago Press, Chicago.

Wormington, H. M., 1957, *Ancient Man in America* (4th ed.), Denver Museum of Natural History, Popular Series No. 4, Denver.

Yen, D. E., 1971, "Construction of the Hypothesis for Distribution of the Sweet Potato," *Man Across the Sea: Problems of Pre-Columbian Contacts,* C. L. Riley, J. C. Kelley, C. W. Pennington, R. L. Rands, editors, University of Texas Press, Austin.

INDEX

155

Monte Albán, 33; carved figures, *49;* developments at, 54; residential area, 48; Teotihuacán features in, 54; Tlatilco elements in, 45
Monumental public construction, 111, 114; *see also* Ceremonial centers
Moran, Hugh, 132
Mordan complex (Hispaniola), 102
Morelos, 41, 44
Mytilus shells, 107

Nahua language, 54
Nazca culture (Peru), 68, 79; trophy head vessel from, *79*
Nicaragua, 29
Nomads, 57, 67, 70
Nordenskiöld, Erland, 131
Northern Plateau, 57
North Patagonia, 89, 91, 105–107

Oaxaca highlands: Maya influences in, 56; Mixtec expansion into, 59; Monte Albán, 51, 54; Olmec economy in, 43; pottery traits, 46; Tehuacán materials in, 35, 51; *see also* Monte Albán
Obsidian, 42, 119
Ocós phase, 33, 39; parallels with Southeast Asia, 39, 45, 133
Olla, 38
Olmeca-Xicalanca, 58–59
Olmec "imperialism," 44, 116; *see also* Olmec tradition
Olmec tradition: characteristics of, 43–44; as civilization, 4, 40, 41, 43, 47; horizon, 40–44; lowland, 46; as Mesoamerican prototype, 41, 43, 57, 116–117; pottery style, 41, 133; in rise of regional cultures, 4, 43–44, 46; Rural Nucleated form of society in, 116; sociopolitical development in, 114
Orinoco Basin, 87, 92–100; manioc cultivation in, 102; pottery of, 96, 98, 100
Oxtotitlán cave paintings, 41

Pachacamac (Peru), 7, 66, 68, 82–83

Palenque (Chiapas), relief with inscriptions from, *55*
Paleoamericans, 11–28; and Eurasian Upper Paleolithic, 26; hunting practices of, 25–26; maritime communities of, 19; skeletal remains of, 13, 19; and transoceanic diffusion, 127
Palli Aike Cave (So. Patagonia), 19, 20, 88, 107
Pampa complex (Peru), 66, 68, 71
Pampas, 89, 105–106
Panoan-speaking peoples, 98, 100
Panpipes, 131
Paper-making, 133–135
Paracas culture (Peru), 68, 76, 78; tie-dying in, 131; transoceanic parallels in, 131
Paraná (Brazil) shellmounds, 104
Patagonia, 11, 13, 87, 89, 91, 105–107
Patlachique phase (Mexico), 32, 48
Peanuts, 76, 126, 141; possible transoceanic diffusion of, 125–126
Percussion-flaked tools, 15, 104, 106
Peru: Chavín spread in, 6; cultivation appears in, 70; early ceramics in, 127; post-Pleistocene artifacts in, 70; pottery-making in, 74; preceramic sites in, 128
Petén, 54; abandonment of, 60; pottery-making, 46
Phillips, Philip, 34
Pijijiapan site (Chiapas), 30, 41
Piki complex (Peru), 20, 21, 70
Pipes, occurrence of, 59, 96
Plantain, pre-Columbian, 126
Plant cultivation: in Andean area, 80–81; in Antilles, 103; by Aztecs, 61; beginnings of, 37, 70, 112–113; in Chihua complex, 71; of chili peppers, 34–35; and civilization, 121; in eastern South America, 89; Flannery on shift to, 36–37; large-scale, on basin floor, 48; Mesoamerican, 34, 35; in the *montaña,* 65; in Olmec culture, 43; origin of, in Mesoamerica, 35; *see also* Agriculture, Irrigation

3 4 5 6 7 8 9 10 11 12 13 14 15   88 87 86 85 84 83 82 81 80 79 78 77 76